BRAVE
FOR
FREEDOM

**THE STORY OF A ROMANIAN REFUGEE AND
HIS JOURNEY TO FLEE HIS COUNTRY**

BRAVE FOR FREEDOM

THE STORY OF A ROMANIAN REFUGEE AND HIS JOURNEY TO FLEE HIS COUNTRY

Jonathan Matei

Copyright © 2022 Jonathan Matei

Limit of Liability/Disclaimer of warranty. This book is designed to provide information, inspiration, and motivation to our readers. It is sold with the understanding that the publisher is not engaged to render any type of legal, psychological, or any other kind of professional advice. The content is the sole expression and opinion of the author, and not necessarily that of the publisher. Neither the publisher nor the individual author(s) shall be liable for any psychological, emotional, physical, financial, or commercial damages, including, but not limited to, incidental, special, consequential or other damages.

Unless otherwise noted, all scripture quotations are taken from the Holy Bible. The Bible translation versions are all listed in the resource page in one of the last pages contained in this book.

All rights reserved. No part of this publication may be reproduced, distributed, or transmitted in any form or by any means, including photocopying, recording, or other electronic or mechanical methods, without the prior written permission of the publisher, except in the case of brief quotations embodied in critical reviews and certain other noncommercial uses permitted by copyright law. For permission requests, write to the publisher, addressed "Attention: Permissions Coordinator," at the address below.

Paperback: 978-1-951475-27-7
Ebook: 978-1-951475-28-4

Library of Congress Control Number: 2023903007
First paperback edition January 2023

Any references to historical events, real people, or real places are used fictitiously. Names, characters, and places are products of the author's imagination.

Cover Art by Amanda Blake Designs

Arrow Press Publishing
245 Pemberly Blvd
Summerville, SC 29486

www.arrowpresspublishing.com

A written memoir about the full life of Viorel Matei, a Romanian refugee, as told to his son, Jonathan Matei.

Table of Contents

Acknowledgments 1

Foreword..4

Preface 6

Buziaș, Romania, 1956 19

The Uprise of Communist Acts, 1958..............................30

The Hardship, Romania, 1960 56

A New Era, 1965 88

Becoming independent, 1973 108

Finding Christ, 1984 121

Fleeing from Romania, 1987..135

Finding the love of my life, 1988 160

The Romanian Revolution, 1989....................................176

ACKNOWLEDGMENTS

To my Lord and Savior, Jesus Christ, whom I love dearly. He is the reason I am living out my American Dream. Jesus Christ is my best friend who has mercy over my life when I least deserve it. Thank you, Jesus.

Special thanks to Pastor Paul Negrut, whom I had the pleasure of meeting back in the early 80s. Paul, thank you for your obedience in honoring the Lord with the words you have spoken to me that day. You led me to Christ at the First Baptist Church, Romania, in 1984. God has gifted you with the remarkable ability to speak and to carry it out efficiently. I was in a terrible place, and your words were compelling and full of life. God loves you, and you have a special place in my heart.

Special thanks to my mother, Minca, who has stood by my side throughout my entire life. Minca, you have seen the best and the worst of me. The saddest days and the happiest days, you never left my side. You were high-strong during the most formidable challenges any woman could imagine. When your husband left for the army, you remained strong and took on the responsibility of caring for us while he was away. I see the core values in your life; you are a strong woman of God, and I love you.

To my grandmother, Stoiana, who took care of me when I was just a little kid and has gone to be with the Lord. You believed I could accomplish my dreams, and you played a significant role in the freedom that I now have. I have always loved staying with you because you provided me with peace and comfort during my most challenging days. Thank you for all that you are. You are missed, and I cannot wait to see you again soon.

I also want to thank Rebecca and Victor Marian for connecting me with Geta, my wife. You two are remarkable and sweet. The Lord has yet to reveal significant blessings in your family. We have a long history of friendship, and words can never express how blessed I am to have known both of you.

To Georghia Marian, who also went to be with the Lord, the father of fourteen kids, including Georgeta, my wife. Thank you for granting me your blessing of marrying your daughter. You have carried a high standard of excellence in your household and have inspired me to do the same for mine. You have set an excellent example of how to lead a God-fearing family, and I admire that about you. I will never forget our conversations, you and me, sitting around the table discussing the Word of God. That conversation took place before I had officially carried a full conversation with Geta, and you play a big part in my life. Thank you again, Georghia.

Special thanks to my wife, Geta. Thank you for being yourself and honest throughout the years. I love your gentle spirit and soft personality. You are my world, and there is nothing more I can ever ask for. I waited patiently until age thirty-five when I saw your beautiful face, the face of peace and love. You stand for what is right in the eyes of God and hold firmly to the values of remaining in his presence. I must say, our marriage has consisted of joy and laughter, even in the midst of chaos. Though we had

Acknowledgments

difficult days trying to raise our kids, you taught me to remain patient while teaching them the right way of life.

This year marks thirty-five years and counting of our happy marriage. I am looking forward to seeing what else God has in store for the both of us. I love you, Geta. And to everyone else who has played a huge part in contributing support after I departed from Romania.

Thank you, Ken, Renee Peterson, Lana, and Marinela Ostheimer, and many more, God bless you all.

FOREWORD

A prefatory comment from the youngest refugee to flee the Romanian country on August 25th, 1979.

As a pastor, for many years I had the privilege to meet many people that had the same trajectory like me. People who love walking on the path of salvation with hope and faith that one day we will be forever with the Lord. One day, a long time ago, I met the Matei family when Jonathan was just a little boy. He was the quiet type, more listening than talking and I always felt something different about him. Time passed and he had grown up and went off to earn himself some education. However, on February 23rd, 2022 at exactly 7:29pm, a young man came knocking on my office door.

A handsome young man wanted to talk with me and wanted me to write a few thoughts on this book that he had written—he has written three books by the way, you should check them out. That young man, a born again christian, now is a writer on christian books about family and helping others to understand the importance of living a godly lifestyle. That young man was Jonathan Matei. What a surprise this was for me, this was a person that was on his way to the path of heaven.

We talked about our native country of Romania and being free after so many years of communism and oppression. When the revolution happened in 1989, I was thinking of saying words of wisdom and packing everything in one paragraph. I found some powerful words in the Bible, words of wisdom, knowledge, and inspiration from King Solomon, the master builder. This is not for a group of some individuals, but for every generation and time. This is not only for Romania but for every country, ethnicity, family, every individual, and now for Jonathan.
Psalms 127:1-2 " Unless the Lord builds the house, the builders labor in vain. Unless the Lord watches over the city, the guards stand and watch in vain."

Jonathan, God is calling you for a special service. I know you enjoy reading quotes written by your favorite church leaders that helped shape you along the way. This is a quote I created: You cannot do God's work without God's help. This distinguishes the difference between success and failure.

Jonathan, I know your family, and I am pleased to hear that you are choosing a good path in life. May God bless you and your future.

Doru Levi Ilioi

PREFACE

Over the course of 25 years, I've had the privilege of befriending Renee Peterson, a successful city mayor in Modesto, California. In 1991, she and many pastors and employers from all over the country were curious as to why I had consistently thought big and dreamt big. They did not realize I had recently fled Romania after a great revolution due to poor economic leadership. It all started after the Soviet Union took power in 1944.

Romania and many other parts of Europe seemed to have no future at the time because of Russia, so I fought to seek freedom and opportunity in the United States. I was hungry for an opportunity. Even more so, I had the never-ending courage to ask around for help. Asking is free.

Friends like Renee and many others periodically had lunch with me at my home, and they would ask me questions like, "What's your story?" I responded, "What do you mean?" They wondered why I was in a rush to seek and find new opportunities in America.

I told them when I lived in Romania, times were tough; there was no future for my family and me. I know friends in Romania who studied long-term to become lawyers and doctors, yet they work in nursing homes, scrubbing toilets. Here in America, there are plenty of opportunities to achieve.

I told Renee and my friends the dream I planned to accomplish here in the States: to set my kids up for success for the future. I spent many countless hours telling my life-story. Years went by, and people still wanted to hear about my life-story; they are curious.

Even today, I frequently invite friends over to my home and have lunch, and they are the ones that spark the question, What's your story? There is something different about you.

I tell them my story. I cannot stop talking, no matter how hard I try. I get fired up and excited to share my passion for freedom with others. I'm sure that many Ukrainian refugees have a story much like mine. I am motivated to share with you that opportunities are real. Communism and national injustice, resulting in the loss of freedom for many people, are things we cannot control.

However, we can control our decisions to be free and find freedom in other countries that allow for better-paying jobs and greater lifestyles for our children. People encouraged me to write a book about my life, especially my daughter, Patricia. I thought it would be a great idea, but I never thought of being an author. I didn't know how to create a book, so I put it off for a while. Then, my son, Jonathan, came to me and said, Tata, I am going to write a book about your life and the revolution. Come, let's plan out the manuscript.

I was amazed and blessed to hear that my son had the motivation to write a book about me. If Jonathan does not write this book, then no one will. So, why should you experience this book? This book contains real-life scenarios and political events that changed Europe forever. It is about a man, who lived in a Soviet-occupied nation, whose national liberty was stolen, but he still dreamt of finding freedom for his family.

I found myself in life-threatening situations time and time again. Only by the grace of God did I manage to survive. The more I tried to escape Romania before the revolution, the more dangerous it became for me. I was very disappointed but never discouraged. I am writing now to inspire you not to take the freedom given to you for granted, because someone paid for it.

Later in my life, I found an amazing church in my hometown in Romania, and sometime later, I surrendered my life to Jesus Christ. My mother, Minca, observed my life up close and gave her life to Jesus after seeing my life thrive. I was imprisoned and beaten for my freedom so that I might have a chance to escape Romania, in its worst state.

Dreaming big is free. Working hard to make freedom a reality is not. I worked hard for my freedom. It all started in World War II When Germany and Romania were no longer allies against Russia, and it all went downhill for Romania. After the war ended, parts of Romania were occupied with Russian soldiers. Romania eventually became a satellite country for Russia.

Communism brought socialism to everyone, and our freedom was taken from us. The rich were stripped of all their farm supplies and animals to support the poor. We had no food because Romania had many national debts to pay off to Russia after the war.

I was born about a decade after World War II ended; It was not a fun place to be. However, it is not how you start, but how you finish.

Listen to or read my story because my journey I am about to share with you is very powerful and impactful to the whole world. At the beginning of this book, you will experience an extended series of thorough dialogue between multiple people up

Preface

to chapter three. This book encompasses my entire life, from the age of three to my late 50s. God bless you as you read or listen to this story.

THE LIFE
of
VIOREL MATEI

PHOTO GALLERY

Photo Gallery

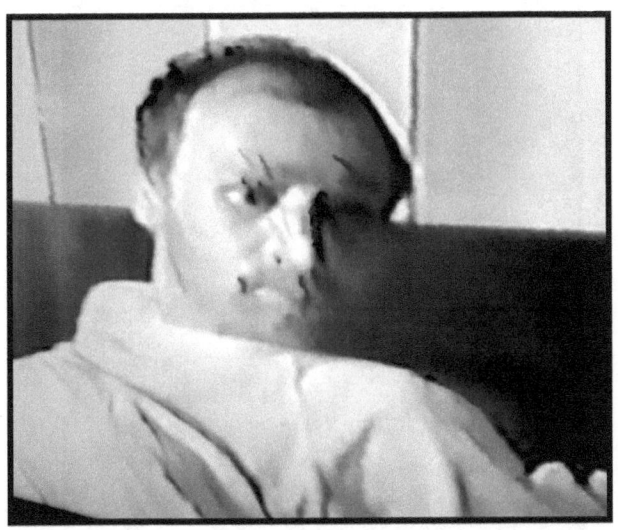

On December 15th, 1989, close to midnight, Viorel was struck by a vehicle while riding his bicycle home from a revival event at his home church. Viorel's face and right leg were severely injured. He was immediately sent to the nearest hospital not knowing that just several hours later, many patients there would be shot dead due to the revolution the following day.

This photo was taken soon after Viorel's father was drafted into the Romanian military on January 30th, 1956. On February 1st that year, during the late rainy evening, his grandma took Viorel out for a night walk around the empty public area downtown. There, Viorel, at the age of two, claims to have experienced his magical moment when he saw a collection of shiny toys behind glass at a closed book store, one of them being an urban rail transit model. This will forever be the memorable and magical night of his childhood.

Photo Gallery

This natural mineral water fountain is called 23rd August. It serves as a memorial after King Michael launched the royal coup on August 23, 1944, causing Romania to change allies in World War II. The King ceased all actions and fought against the Axis powers. The entire country was then occupied by the Red Army soon after when no armistice offer was accepted. This piece is also the most majestic, impressive, and famous fountain in all of Buziaș and in the entire world. This is one of three mineral fountains located in Buziaș: Mos Bazies and Felix. Springing up from the ground comes never-ceasing fresh cold water completely saturated in high quantities of minerals such as magnesium, calcium, and sodium. This low-pressure carbonated mineral water comes highly recommended by many doctors all across the country for those who need medical attention, especially for those with heart conditions. Thirst quencher and healing are guaranteed to those who find this fountain, only located in Buziaș.

In 1965, Viorel paid his parents a visit to a farm town they were staying at, during the summer after living with his Grandmother. It was then when he became mesmerized by the new television Dad had purchased—televisions were new and rare in those days. He also spent a good deal of time with his cousin Marcela and his brother, exploring the village, its agriculture, and the cows. On Sunday-fun days, the three of them including my sister went out to pull mulberries and plums from the trees out in the fields as their fun ritual. They enjoyed some time playing hide-and-seek, as well as climbing trees for fun.

Photo Gallery

Patients who have been given natural mineral water to treat their medical condition, especially heart conditions, come here to this hotel to rest for the night. Viorel's Mother worked as a housekeeper in Buziaş. While his Grandmother worked here as a chef to provide food and hospitality to those staying here. This hotel was a life-saver for both his mother and grandmother as they were undergoing a difficult financial crisis due to Dad drafting into the military with no notice and no government financial aid.

Viorel during the 70s. By this time he found a reliable job as a lathe operator in Timișoara, Romania.

The wedding of Georgeta and Viorel, 1988

BUZIAŞ, ROMANIA, 1956

My name is Viorel Matei. I was born July 5, 1953 in Buziaş, Romania, and on March 29, 1991, I fled my country.

I do not understand why people take freedom for granted when it has been handed to them. When you purchase freedom, you have all the reasons in the world to protect it. Nothing is free. Even if it is freely given to you, someone must pay for it. That was my motto growing up in the old western part of Buziaş, Romania.

Even in my earliest years, I became content with what I had at three years old. I had everything I needed. I had my father Stefan, my mother Minca, my sister Rodica, and my brother Vasile, as well as a strong urge for freedom inside of me.

Times were very uncertain, and it only worsened as my childhood began. My dad was the only breadwinner and kept the family in one piece so that we could survive. Although the bond between my dad and I was not very strong, just when I thought I could grow closer to him and build a friendship, the worst happened.

On January 30th, 1956, he received a letter from the Romanian army stating that he must report to the recruiting center for a few quick questions. I did not see this as a good sign, considering the Russians were bringing communism to Romania. Something was up.

I was too young to understand what communism was or what it was doing in Romania, so for your sake as the reader, I will describe it as though I did understand it.

"Where is Dad going?" I asked myself, as I observed the dreadful rise of ruin approaching. I thought he went to do something important, but I did not know what was happening.

My brother was in a continuous mood swing as we all waited for dinner. We were all very thankful to have enough food to survive. Starvation was common within our household. Every day I pondered how delightful it would be to go to bed with a full stomach. And though that rarely happened, I was even more concerned for my brother and sister's wellbeing.
As much as I dreamt of eating at a dining table filled with soft buttered bread with hot soup, I always shared with my siblings when they needed more food and when I had any extra food left over.

It became almost normal to go to bed on an empty stomach, a terrible experience! Going to sleep and not knowing where the next meal would come from was difficult for my siblings and me. It made our lives so much harder, especially since Dad left with such short notice.

We used kerosene-powered lamps to tell stories before bed and spent quality family time together at night. My family remained united and strong throughout the problematic tragedies we faced. Nothing could have taken us apart. I am incredibly thankful for my mom because she constantly ran back and forth across the house to meet our needs while we were helpless and hungry kids.

My mom did her best to keep us calm during a fateful night like this. But one day, Stoiana, my only grandmother, visited for a day and spent time with me. It was an unforgettable night for me. On February 1, 1956, I couldn't stop crying because of the difficult conditions at home. My grandma took me by the hand, and we walked around the open public square in downtown Buziaş. We stopped to see the August 23 mineral water fountain on our way there.

This majestic fountain, one of three original mineral water fountains in Buziaş, stands about four feet tall and is located in the center of a nearby park, not too far from where I lived. This sculpture is one of the most beautiful things I have ever seen as a child. I could not believe the fresh, low-pressure carbonated water straight from the ground sprung up for me to drink. It was not artificial; this cold water continuously flows deep underground and never ceases. It contains many minerals, such as sodium, calcium, and magnesium. This sublime water gives out a glorious fragrance, a whiff of iron, and a natural, earthy scent like you've never experienced before. Many who drink this water say it benefits the internal organs, primarily the stomach, and it is a great thirst quencher.

People who drink this water must drink it immediately to get the best tasteful experience. Otherwise, if you save the water in a water bottle for the next day, it will not taste good. This fountain has been active for hundreds of years, constantly pulling water from underground without stopping—It still stands today.

Grandma smiled as she watched me, mesmerized by what I saw and drank. Now I know why they called this Fountain August. It is majestic and famous all around the country. I stayed near the fountain a little longer, enjoying the carbonated bubble sensation washing down my throat. Then we continued our walk during the night. She held my hand throughout the entire walk on the wet sidewalk path. I couldn't help but jump over the little rain puddles. I always got so excited because I wanted to make it to the other side of the puddle. Grandma would laugh and say, "Why are you being so silly tonight, little boy?"

I guess I was behaving as every little boy behaves. I will never forget that walk Stoiana and I had downtown on the dark, cold night. That gave me great comfort because she was positive, despite her own personal affairs, other people were her priority.

As we were walking, something caught my attention. I looked to my left to see a large, long building with glass walls and lights that lit up the street corners. One store, a bookstore, sold toys on an open display. It was all concealed by the glass wall, but it was closed. I admired a shiny toy from afar, a tramvai, meaning an urban rail transit toy. So, I ran towards it.

Christmas had just passed, but I still felt the Christmas spirit when I saw this toy. I wanted that toy, so I asked Grandma to get it for me; I would do anything for it. I had fixed my eyes on that toy for such a long time. Grandma noticed that, too. I was not able to stop looking at it and thinking about it. Grandma planned to buy that toy for me on Christmas day sometime soon. I did not know it, but she wanted to surprise me. I did not get that toy that night, but I knew I would someday get it.

We went back home, and soon Grandma had to go back home to her place. My sister, brother, and I gathered around my mother as she told us stories. She was a terrific storyteller. Some were funny stories; others were the kind that helped us fall asleep before bedtime.

Mom brought us to the kitchen one morning to feed us what she had in the cabinets. She held a spoon in one hand filled with honey and carried my younger brother in the other arm. She rocked my brother on her arm as she walked around the kitchen in her sunflower swing dress.

On the floor with tired eyelids, ready to take my daily nap, Mom received the word from the recruiting center in the mail. I couldn't help but listen as Mom silently read the post leader. My heart was beating faster and harder as I anticipated her reaction to the postcard. My sister and I were so confused because we did not know what was going on. This was so unexpected and unplanned.

Then my mother's facial expression gradually changed as she finished the letter. She slowly placed the card on the table and staggered down the hallway to her bedroom.

"This is too much for me," Mom cried out with teary eyes while distressfully dropping her spoon of honey on the floor and then setting Vasile down.

Uncertainty permeated the entire atmosphere of our home and hearts with the news, especially after Mom exploded with distress. I can remember the feeling of hopelessness, fear, and anger because of the fraud that has taken place. No one was able to get a hold of my dad. My dad was unable to contact us either.

As I approached my mother's bedroom, I held on to my teddy bear for extra security. After my dad was taken away, I deeply desired to protect my family. I did the best I could to support my sister and my brother. Some chores had to be done, and food had to be made. I intended to do some simple chores and make food for my family to ease the tension in our household.

Though I did my best, there was nothing much I could do because we had run short on finances for about two weeks. The army was not concerned about our welfare and finances. The communists in Romania had a lot of power. They did whatever they wanted without reason. This shows how terrible communism can be. They steal and destroy what is yours. In this case, they needed my dad for the army and just left us for dead.

Ever since my dad was taken away, I made it my mission to someday escape from this country and fight for freedom. I was distraught with the communist movement in Romania because the leaders did not care about you; they only cared for themselves. That made my childhood so much harder. I was only a three-year-old child, left without a father. I was lonely without my father.

My grandma, an honest and loving communist, came to our house and gave us some food to eat. She took care of us and comforted Mom in her disappointment. She brought us many toys and candy. If Grandma had known sooner, she would have come faster, but she did not know what happened until recently. We were so happy and thankful to see her. She was full of joy and cheer.

She helped me understand that joy and peace can exist even in the darkest and loneliest moments. Grandma stayed at our home for a few days to grieve and provide for us. She then offered to take us to her home to live with her for a while.

We all thought it was a great idea to escape this dark atmosphere and move to a different place for a time. We left for Strada Eminescu in Buziaș and stayed there for quite a while. We found ourselves moving from one city to another, so we spent quite a bit of time in each city before moving again.

I was amazed at all the green fields and wildflowers covering the valley's foothills. It was the most beautiful view I had ever seen. When I walked into her home, I was introduced to someone who had become fatherless about two years before. Being shy and timid, I turned to my grandma and said, "Who is that girl in the living room?"

"She is your aunt," Grandma replied. Do not mention anything about your father, okay? Grandma insisted in a hushed tone.

"Why not?" I asked. "Just don't, not until later. She is not in a good place right now," Grandma told me.

Zoia was eight years old. Her father, Dirmon, died. He was a communist party secretary, and he held much power in the town of Giarmata, Romania. Most people who lived in the town of Giarmata were a German minority. They would try to bribe Dirmon with fresh eggs, chicken, vegetation, and other possessions. But Dirmon was very honest and refused those offers because he wanted to do deals the right way, not with fraud. He was the only prominent leader in that area who was against corruption and communism. Then, he suddenly died from brain cancer.

"Where is this country headed? Nothing is getting better around here," Zoia said. She suspected the communist leaders poisoned her father because he was only forty-six years old. Things seemed very suspicious.

"What did I tell you?" shouted Grandma towards me.

"What!? I didn't say anything," I replied defensively. "I told you not to tell Zoia about your father, and now she is reminded of her father's death!" Grandma shouted.

I ran to a room, closed the door behind me, and stayed there because my first impression of Zoia was ruined. It turned out that Zoia overheard our quiet conversation about not mentioning my father to her. It triggered her. Zoia left the house for some fresh air and went to seek financial support from the government as she had planned since yesterday.

Though communism began in 1944 with the power of Stalin, the corruption did not take effect until the early 1950s. Well, here we are, towards the end of 1958, and things were changing rapidly. I felt terribly upset about Zoia's condition because I understood how she felt, left without a father. Seeing Zoia for the first time did not turn out the way I wanted, but I was glad we had some common ground. Both of us had fathers who left us.

"Have a chat with Zoia when she gets back; she may need some comfort," Grandma instructed.

"Sure thing! I understand her pain," I replied.

I was amazed at how my grandma was so loving to my family, especially after losing her husband. She is very selfless and caring, right after a devastating cause, I thought to myself as I made my way around the house. Though I had a great time staying at my grandma's house, she was unemployed. She wouldn't talk about her financial problems much because she was more concerned about us not having a place to stay.

While playing with my toys, I heard Grandma mention she wanted to buy bread the following day. Mom replied, "You don't have money for bread. Besides, good luck trying to find some; bread is hard to find."

"I can wake up early tomorrow morning, rush to the market and be first in line," Grandma replied.

The meager wages complicated living, and it was challenging to buy food, especially with no income. I dreamt of being fortunate enough to walk into a store and shop for whatever I wanted. Mom had to be super thrifty to purchase the food she needed for the week. Mom went shopping for bread, honey, and tomatoes. We ate plenty of honey during this time. It was very fresh, and that was what we had at the time. We used honey to soothe sore-throat pains and applied some to our tea with a little bit of lemon juice while eating tomato with bread. That was a healthy option, cheap, and a great way to stay healthy.

Hunting for food became a daily routine for our family. You would expect someone like me to get used to this lifestyle by age five. I was content, but still frustrated with our lifestyle. I thought there must be a better life out there somewhere. I just need to find it. No matter how tough life was, my grandma and Mom comforted me all the time.

After Mom spent about five hours looking around for cheap deals on bread and honey, we were astonished she managed to get it. Grandma took the bread that morning, spread honey over it, and started singing while feeding my siblings and me. I will never forget it.

Grandma had ways with rhymes and melodies as she sang; it was very intriguing. Breakfast was my favorite part of the day because we always gathered to eat and spend quality time together. Nothing is better than family bonding. It created such a positive atmosphere for me when I had loving people around me.

Speaking of positivity, Grandma sought financial support, and the government issued her a pension. She received this pension due to her father's death to support her family. Grandma and Mom were unemployed. This pension was the only stream of income flowing into our household. To feed and support an entire family with a tiny pension was not easy. It provided some money for us to get by. We had six mouths to feed, but at least we had something consistently supporting us.

Grandma also helped Mom financially so she could purchase food without worrying. Grandma and Mom decided to shop for food early in the morning to buy more meat, bread, and milk.

I woke up early on the morning of February 18, and it was scalding outside. I was surprised that it would be this hot in the early morning. I remember sleeping during the night, and it was tough for me to sleep because I was sweating heavily at night. We relied on the little fan that we had to stay cool. It did not help much, but it was all we had.

With no wind outside, only a heatwave, I continued to sweat even more during the day. It seemed too dangerous to go out that morning. Mom had no choice but to go out to find bread, and we were very short on food and milk.

"Grandma! Mom! Where are you two going? Can't you see it is too hot?" I shouted.

"Stay still. We will be back. We will wait in line to get food first. It will be quick," Mom encouraged.

Grandma and Mom had left. I do not understand how they would go out during 105-degree weather in an attempt to buy food for the family. As I watched the terrible weather from inside the house, at least a breeze started to pick up.

While Mom and Grandma took off to buy food, my sister, brother, and I went outside to play hide-and-seek. We went to hide somewhere far off in the field. There were hundreds of trees all around our home. I stayed beside my brother to watch over him because he was only a year old. We both hid behind a Fagus Sylvatica tree. I wanted to climb this tree, but unfortunately, I didn't know how. I was a bit chubby as a kid and did not want to risk falling so hard from this tree.

I shot my brother a double-take, "What are you doing?" My brother appeared to be a hyper child with very little control and was tough to deal with. He tried to climb a tree; obviously, he couldn't because he was too small. His attempt was funny because he kept falling on the dirty ground.

I stumbled upon a thick piece of wood partially covered by thatch. I lost my balance and fell on my back. I was trying to get back up, but I noticed a plane soaring high in the sky. Planes have always intrigued me. "'Rodica!", I shouted with excitement. She could not hear me, so I took some dirt and tried throwing it at my sister to get her attention.

"We were not here to get dirt on ourselves," my sister said.

Buziaș, Romania, 1956

That plane had already passed, but I saw another aircraft fly across the sky.

"Look at that plane!" I said while pointing at the sky. "Someday, I will fly to America on that plane."

My sister responded with a scoff, "You think everything in life is possible, don't you?"

I have desired to live in America ever since I saw that plane ripping through the skies so freely. I made it my mission to someday fly to America and become a citizen. I believed I would eventually be free from the life of communism.

Zoia and I continued playing as we entered the house. I thought to myself, "I hope Grandma and Mom are okay out there." They had been gone for about two hours. I kept thinking about them because I thought something had happened to them. I was a bit worried because they took much longer than I expected.

Suddenly, we all heard the door slowly crack open. We're home! Mom announced enthusiastically. And we have great news.

As Grandma and Mom struggled to carry multiple bags of fresh food inside, Mom said, "Not only do we have plenty of bread, meat, and honey, but we also have some special news!"

"What is the good news?" my sister asked, as she ran to give Mom a huge hug. "I will tell everyone tomorrow during breakfast because it's getting late." She replied.

"Mom, we were all worried. You took such a long time to get back," my sister replied. "Well, it is because your grandma and I met someone today, and you'll be happy to hear the news tomorrow!"

My sister responded with joy and excitement, "I am so happy you're finally home. I can't wait to hear the good news tomorrow!"

2

THE UPRISE OF COMMUNIST ACTS, 1958

The sun began to set. The children had been sound asleep for about an hour by now. Mom contacted her new employer regarding tomorrow's work schedule.

"Let me wash your work clothes for tomorrow," Grandma whispered.

"Please, do it quickly; the water shuts off in fifteen minutes," Mom responded quietly.

Mom and Grandma communicated from across the house while trying not to wake up the kids. They can't contain their excitement; they finally have a job.

New opportunities were opening up for this family, and we stayed content. We did not have any other options because of our current circumstances.

"We need to be at work at 5 a.m. to start," Mom said to Grandma. Grandma and Mom became very excited about her new job. The economy has been falling apart, and many families have been unemployed. This was fascinating news.

Mom and Grandma woke us up at 4 a.m. and shared the good news with us as they prepared a very early breakfast.

My sister, my brother, Zoia, and I were amazed at how quickly this happened. A few days ago, Grandma and Mom were jobless, searching for food out in the cold. Now, they both have jobs.

I was curious how they managed to receive employment so quickly, so I had to ask Grandma for more information.

"Grandma, how did you get this job? She explained that while she and Mom were at the grocery store that morning, they overheard a man in front of them in line to purchase our food. He talked to someone in front of him about his employees at a hotel just a few blocks away. The man's name was Andrew.

"It was frigid out," Grandma said. So, she couldn't help but talk to the man ahead of her. "Standing around and not talking to people will make me freeze to death." Grandma dared to tell this man that she and Mom both needed jobs.

"Why are you coming to me with this question? Many people are waiting to get this job, too," Andrew told her.
Grandma's first impression of Andrew was not good at all. He seemed to be in a hurry, and he was also vulgar.

"Look! We both need jobs. We have mouths to feed, my husband is deployed, and we have low income from a pension." Grandma was not ashamed to say it to his face. Grandma continued to talk to Andrew about their situation.

Andrew happened to be the shift supervisor at the nearby Grand Hotel kitchen. This hotel attracts many guests and patients, particularly those with cardiovascular problems. Some people who stay at this hotel are given treatment for their diseases by using carbonated mineral water.

"I'll tell you what," Andrews stated, "I will give you a chance since you both are bold." Andrew saw how sincere Grandma and Mom were.

Shortly after their conversation, Andrew built a small connection with them. He allowed them to come into work on a day that worked best for them. The only available positions were the chef and housekeeper, as every other job had been taken.

"Come in a couple of days, and I will try to see what I can do for you two," Andrew said.

"Thank you, thank you! You don't understand how badly we need these jobs," Mom told him.

As Mom and Grandma eventually received food in line and began to walk away, Andrew turned and said, "Also, thank you for being bold and asking; most people who are not bold are in last place," Andrew said.

I was excited to hear Grandma explain how they received this opportunity. In the beginning, Andrew was rude, but he slowly connected with Mom and Grandma while they talked in line.

Mom said she would work as a hotel housekeeper, and I would be a chef. We will help treat some hotel patients by making food."

Mom said her sister should be here in about 5 minutes to babysit us, kids, here at home. Although I had never met my aunt, I wanted to meet her for the first time.

Grandma turned to me and said, "Viorel, I want you to watch over your brother, sister, and Zoia. Keep them out of trouble."

I told Grandma I would do that, but I did not understand why I had to watch over them since my aunt, who I hadn't met, was coming to babysit us. *I might have them do my chores around the house then.*

The Uprise of Communist Acts, 1958

While Mom and Grandma went off to work at the hotel nearby, my aunt arrived with chocolate and snacks for all of us. She had the biggest smile on her face and was very approachable and friendly. We always loved having her over to stay at our house. "Thank you!

"Thank you!" I said as I opened the chocolate bars. I have always loved Romanian chocolate, especially the ones with peanuts inside. The house became loud with plenty of chatter as everyone rushed to see my aunt and hug her.

"Îmi pregătesc mâncarea și apoi vom merge cu toții să ne jucăm afară," my aunt said in Romanian.

Shortly after she arrived, there was mail at the door. I went to pick up the mail to see what was inside.

"I will hold onto this mail until your mom gets home," my aunt said. I was eager to open that letter to see if it was from ad. "Grandma will open it when she comes home. Go on. To the kitchen, both of you," she said.

My sister, brother, Zoia, and I helped her prepare lunch. My aunt purchased all the necessary food. Over several hours, we watched my aunt make *ardei umpluți*, or stuffed bell peppers. This dish has always been my favorite food of all time. Nothing can compare with this delicious dish.

I helped my aunt fill the red bell peppers with delicious ground beef and dice the garlic cloves. I've come to believe I cannot live without garlic cloves. It is one of the best flavoring agents for any food, like soups, stews, meats, and more.

I made sure the bell peppers were packed entirely with extra juicy beef before cooking them in the heat. My brother and my sister prepared the rice and cheese. Zoia was in charge of seasoning everything, which was an easy job, but for some reason, she kept putting extra olive oil in the mix when we only needed six tablespoons to complete everything. She spilled some extra oil in the mix, and ever since then, I have always given her a hard time.

During dinner, I needed a glass of water. But instead, I asked Zoia for something else, "Hey Zoia, can you give me a cold glass of olive oil." My brother and I would burst out laughing, while my aunt told me to knock it off. Zoia would have flashbacks of spilling oil in the beef mix and crying. I guess I could be a bully sometimes, but I tried to stop.

I enjoyed helping my aunt cook because I felt a part of the preparation. She wanted us to cook; she always loved having us around.

The red stuffed peppers came out nice and juicy. Extra red juice filled up the peppers' surrounding area, and it smelt so warm and delicious. It took us at least five hours to prepare the delightful, warm stuffed red bell peppers because we were also chattering and fooling around as we usually do.

As we put all the ingredients and dishes away, my aunt told us that half the battle was washing dishes, which is also part of the cooking process. I kept that in mind as I tried learning from her footsteps while cleaning up.

"Where is the olive oil glass?" my aunt asked. I responded with a smirk, "I threw it away. It was empty."

Zoia threw an oven mitt at me, "Will you cut it out!"

"That's enough, Viorel!" my aunt scolded me.

"I'm just joking, jeez! I put it in the pantry!"

We stored the leftover stuffed red bell peppers for the next day. I pondered the past few days as I cleaned up the table and washed the floor. Thankfulness filled my heart as I watched my siblings playing around the house and realized we had food stored away for the next day.

My Mom and Grandma were both at work, earning money to pay the bills. *It cannot get any better than this,* I thought to myself.

Though my aunt was taking care of us while Mom and Grandma were away at work, I still wanted to care for my sister, Vasila, and Zoia, to ensure they were healthy and safe.

My aunt saw how responsible I was cleaning the house and putting together simple foods for my sister, Vasila, and Zoia. I remember my aunt telling me that I had something special ahead of me in life–great things. She told me always to work hard to achieve what I want in life, never give up, and always fight for what I want. So, I asked her how she managed to find food at stores during these difficult times in Romania.

She told me, "Knock, and the door will be opened for you; keep asking, and you shall receive."

"Where did you hear that from," I asked.

She told me this passage comes from Matthew 7:7 in the Bible. I did not know much about the Bible and how to apply it to my everyday life. I hardly read the Bible, and we do not talk about it much at home. However, we would pray and read the Bible whenever Grandma did so.

We were all finishing up and getting ready for bed, and suddenly, I heard some noise from outside. Some sort of chatter, and the front door opened. Mom and Grandma had returned from a long day of work.

"Mom!" I exclaimed as I ran to hug her. My sister and Zoia mentioned the letter to Grandma. My aunt handed the letter to Grandma as she prepared to return to her house.

I wanted her to open it because it had been a while since we heard from Dad. "Alright, stand back, kids. Let me have space to read," Grandma said.

The letter from the army communicated that my dad would be discharged from the military and come home on January 30th, 1958. Everyone cheered and shouted with joy as Grandma read the letter aloud. Mom began to cry. She could hardly wait to see my dad again.

"The army took my husband away, and he never came to visit or talk by letter." Mom said. It was tough for our family to have my dad gone for so long. It is a blessing to have him back to have our family bonds and grow as a family.

"When will Dad come home?" I asked Grandma.

"Tomorrow morning" she said.

It was a massive relief for everyone to have a father figure and financial supporter back home. Before Dad left, I wanted to grow my friendship with him, but the military took him away two years ago. I could hardly wait to start over and enjoy my time with my dad.

I wondered how my dad felt while he was away from us. He could have experienced emotional anxiety because he might not know how to react around us after being gone for so long. As I've gotten older and become a man myself, I realized the chances of him spending time with us might be slim only because of the stress he carried from serving in the army.

So, I told Grandma and Mom I wanted to return to our other home and prepare the house for him. It was quite the commute to the other home as it was in a different city, so I had to make it work. I wanted to have a gathering at Dad's house to greet him with a warm welcome back party.

I was also happy to hear that we could finally afford to buy food and prepare for my dad's arrival.

Grandma had a great idea for finding more food for a lower price. Grandma's co-worker, Ana, knows the head chef who manages the food distribution downtown. She quickly left the house to meet with Ana to find the chef and buy food faster. The head chef would be able to help us receive more food for much cheaper than having to go to the store and pay more money.

My entire family was filled with excitement as Grandma left to meet the head chef because she was building connections with other people to shop for extra food for a lower price. A good relationship with good people was the primary way of shopping and receiving additional fresh foods. Having enough money for food is a blessing because now I do not have to go to bed and think about where the next meal will come from.

Mom wanted to clean my dad's house for his arrival tomorrow morning. Even though Mom and Grandma had to work early the next morning, they tried hard to find food and prepare a party for tomorrow.

The following day, the whole family went to Dad's house in Recas, which was located in a small cow farm, to clean. We quickly prepared the food and drinks. Grandma went out to buy fresh bread, tomatoes, and other ingredients for a great price yesterday. We had plenty of food, and we were very thankful to have known the head chef at the distribution center. We now have a huge table full of fresh food for cheap.

As we prepared the house, my sister yelled loudly, "He's here! He is outside!"

Dad's recruiter dropped him off, and he started walking into his house without knowing we had set up a surprise gathering for him. As soon as Dad opened the door to enter, we all jumped up very loudly, full of excitement and cheer.

"Welcome home!" Mom shouted with tears in her eyes.

"Is this my early birthday celebration," Dad asked.

"Dad, we have been waiting for you to come home, so we threw a celebration to welcome you back," I told him excitedly.

I cannot express the joy I felt when my dad returned home. It is so great to have a complete family again. As I originally shared, having Dad away from the family was heartbreaking because I needed a father figure in my life. *I thought things should definitely improve now that Dad is home, and he will also start working again and provide for us.*

But my sister and I felt a bit suspicious of Dad's behavior around the house just a few hours after he arrived. He seemed very excited to see his entire family at home, but something did not seem right. I went to my room to speak with my sister and Zoia about Dad's behavior. He seems a bit off.

However, my sister felt he was just worn down from serving in the military for two years.

I thought, *maybe she could be right. Dad needs to adjust with us for a few days, and everything will return to normal.*

Later I asked Mom why Dad was acting a bit angry and uneasy. I just did not understand.

"Your father is stressed trying to find a job as a mechanic, that's all. It's just a rough transition," Mom told me.

I knew there had to be something more than that because he seemed very controlling and demanding every day. Dad acted this way before he went into the military, but now it seemed worse.

I felt very disappointed. Living the last few years without my dad, I had high expectations for what it would be like when he returned. I felt distraught by his behavior.

Since Dad's return, an atmosphere of anger and rage filled the house. I wanted a father figure to influence me as a child, but everything seemed to be going in the opposite direction.

One day, I came out of my room and ran excitedly to Dad. I planned on telling him that my birthday was coming up next week. Running through the halls towards the kitchen, I heard a

The Uprise of Communist Acts, 1958

constant commotion in the kitchen. Dad and Mom were arguing and babbling incoherently about the rise of communist activity in Buziaş and other cities.

As I came to the kitchen to hug my dad and tell him of my birthday coming up, he physically abused Mom, and she fell to the floor.

I could not believe my eyes. Mom was on the floor. Trying to get up, short of breath and crying, she looked at Dad.

Then Dad looked at me and said, "Don't just stand here. Go to your room."

I quickly ran to my mom to protect her. "She did not deserve this!" I yelled at Dad.

"Run to your room," Mom said, still crying.

I did not want to leave the kitchen with Mom alone. I wanted to protect her; she was everything to me. I stood beside her and tried to help her up.

Dad came toward me, dragged me away, and beat my joints harshly with a 10-inch wooden stick until I wasn't able to move. The pain was so bad I struggled to breathe. He then left my room to go to Minca in the kitchen. I limped for weeks after the beating he gave me, and I secretly cried every night because I thought he would attack me again.

"Leave her alone; she is not the problem!" I shouted at my dad. I was shaking and crying.

Grandma, my sister, Zoia, and my brother were all in another room filled with distress. They heard it all too. I ran to Grandma and asked her to help Mom in the kitchen. Grandma said she did not want to get in between them; they needed to sort things out.

"My sister! What do we do?" I asked, trembling.

"I do not know. Suddenly, this man has lost his mind," my sister said.

I stayed in the one bedroom with my other siblings and waited for the argument to de-escalate. My brother busted my door open, yelling, "Viorel! Dad will not stop arguing with Mom in the kitchen!" My brother and I went to the kitchen to try to calm Dad down.

Mom told Dad, "Just tell me what is going on. I only want to know."

"The Regime! Minca! The Russian Regime!" Dad yelled at Mom.

"What about the Russian Regime?" Mom asked.

"The communist government has been affecting my job. They took all my personal equipment and claimed it as theirs," Dad said.

"Ever since the Russians invaded this country, the Romanian communists are changing everything," Dad continued.

My dad spent a lot of money on farming equipment and gears to repair his tractors a couple of years before leaving for the military. The government took all of his belongings and placed them in the state warehouse. The warehouse was called "GAS" for Gospodaria Agricola De Stat. The Regime's governmental power, enforced by Stalin in Russia, took over the entire eastern block of Europe. Countries like Germany, Bulgaria, Hungary, Poland, and others suffered significant losses as the Russian communist power took farmland, animals, supplies, and whatever they wanted away from rich people. The Regime confiscated them all and brought them all to the State Farm. There everyone shared the same equipment and farm supplies. No one was allowed to own anything anymore.

This was why my dad became furious. It was not so bad before he left for the army; when he returned from the army, it had worsened. My dad could not stand this happening. Now he has to go to the State Farm to work as a tractor-driver using the government's property equipment, which used to belong to other people.

The communist power became worse and worse every year. Due to the communist Regime, the government also wanted to enforce the Cooperativa Agricola de Productie (CAP). CAP was the socialist activity to take supplies, land, animals, and more away from peasants so that everyone must share the same supplies. This began in 1945 and continued until the 1960s.

My dad was against this movement, and he was not able to stand this any longer. With Dad known to have anger issues, we were all trying to help him calm down. Zoia took Mom to the other room to settle down. Grandma talked to Dad about his concerns.

Dad began to tell Grandma about his new job as a tractor mechanic in the town of Remetea Mare, located northwest of Buziaş. There, he would work to repair tractors and many other machines in a state farm shop. The tractors would then be sent out to the farms.

He would travel to Bucovat, an agricultural village in Romania located just west of Buziaş, 31 kilometers away. He planned on moving our entire family into a small, old shabby house, much closer to his new job in the town of Remetea Mare. He would commute almost four kilometers on his bicycle daily for work.

He wanted to own his own tractor, but he could not. The communist government officials took all supplies, tractors, and animals away from the rich and the middle class and stored everything in a state farm shop at Remetea Mare.

The family would move in about four months. Before we moved, Dad took me to Sacosu Turcesc, a town located west of Buziaş. We traveled by a little carriage pulled by a horse.

Once we arrived, my dad met with some of his friends and introduced me to them. Dad wrapped his arms around me to show his love for me.

For some reason, he placed his palm over my face as the horse pulled us along. I was not able to see the town and its beauty. We stayed there for some time before returning to Buziaș to prepare for our move.

"Having my family back again would be great," Dad said, "Besides, there is a middle school nearby for Viorel."

I realized my dad had much more respect for me while I was with him in Sacosu Turcesc. I began to look forward to moving.

As I packed my things, I wondered why my brother did not want to move. I thought he wanted to.

We did not have a choice. He ran into his room because he was upset about moving away from Buziaș.

"Come on, Vasile," Grandma said. "Come out of the room. Why don't you want to leave to see the new village? You will have a great time there."

My brother was afraid that Dad might make him work with him at Remetea Mare.

"You won't be working with me. You will stay and go where I go," Dad said. I will probably take Viorel with me as an assistant because he is much older.

Dad wanted us to pack quickly and carry our necessities, which should not be much. I was told that we would be traveling from village to village from here on out after we moved to this village, and I would build more friendships along the way. I was excited about the nearby middle school I could attend, within walking distance from where I would be staying. Dad may have me help in the field after school because he wanted to teach me what it meant to work hard. I sensed Dad was trying to rebuild his relationship with all of us. We all thought we might as well give him a chance.

I had all my things packed up and ready to leave Buziaș. I want to be around my father and spend some time with him. I just hoped he would remain calm for a while and not burst into anger again.

I only wanted to go live with my grandma instead because he physically abused my mom right before my eyes. I loved my mom, and I never wanted to see her get hurt. I really hoped Dad wouldn't become angry with me suddenly during our new stay, or else I knew I would try to live with my grandma. However, I decided to trust the process and see what happened.

In the late spring of 1959, that night before I prepared to leave, I spent a lot of time with Grandma because I knew I wouldn't see her for a while.

Dad woke us up early in the morning and said," Hurry up; let's go so we can go and get to work."

It was first come, first serve in the Remetea Mare state farm warehouse, and many peasant farmers came in early at noon to take the best supplies. My dad knew when you showed up late to the shop, only the broken, rusty, inadequate equipment remained.

The main reason why many mechanics took the best tractors and equipment was that they kept busy as required by the government. The communist government wanted people to stay active so they wouldn't have time to think or talk about the evil Regime.

My mom and my siblings decided to go to the shabby old house my dad had rented while my dad and I went straight to his warehouse. Dad was a mechanic; he repaired all sorts of tractors. We made it to the State Farm warehouse, so he needed to test-drive them out around the Remetea Mare area so that when farmers eventually drove them in the fields, they would work very well, so he wanted to leave early to find the best tractor.

We sat down on this stone bench in this huge Remetea garage shop. The shop was quite dirty, unmaintained, and smelled very bad. The communists owned this warehouse.

Dad sat beside me, preparing his gear for work. I asked him if he had apologized to Mom.

"Apologize? For what?" Dad scoffed, and he turned his head away.

"You know what you did, Dad; you know exactly what happened in that kitchen yesterday when you hit Mom because you were angry!" I yelled, "Two and a half years I have waited for you. Your whole family missed you. Is this what you bring to the table?"

Dad became angry, but I wanted to know if he apologized and why he abused Mom.

"Stay in your lane, Viorel; this is not your problem. Have some respect for your father," Dad said to me.

"If you love Mom, then you also love us. You did not apologize, did you?" I asked again in a whisper.

"Dad, I have always wanted to build a connection with you, even before you left for the army. I've always wanted to be near you, but now this is getting in the way," I responded with assertiveness.

Even as a little kid, I was not afraid to speak out and tell my dad the truth.

Dad turned his head towards me and slapped me in the face. "This is my affair, not yours. You want to bond. We will bond while we work. Come on; let's go," he said.

Shortly after this, Mom, my sister, and my brother arrived at Bacova, settling down at Dad's home.

The Uprise of Communist Acts, 1958

Dad gave me tasks to accomplish. He wanted me to learn what labor was from a very young age. It was about 95 degrees outside during the hot summer. Dad handed me a 54-inch, wood-handle action hoe and sent me to a small grass field to create a dirt path. It was so hot outside; my shirt became heavy from sweat after three hours of work.

"That's right! Keep it up," Dad yelled out from a distance.

"Am I the only one who will work hard? What about my brother? Bring him here too, not just me," I complained out loud.

"Oh, do not worry. He will join you tomorrow, and it will be even hotter then," Dad replied.

I wanted a father figure in my life. I expected to play physical sports with Dad in Bacova, not work on difficult tasks.

"What? Are you crying now? You have a runny nose too?" Dad tried to shame me.

"It's just allergies, Dad. It's fine," I replied. This transition from Buziaș to this new village was difficult because of the friction between my dad and me. I really wanted to go back to Buziaș and live with Grandma. My brother should have been working with me here in the fields, too.

Ever since Dad came, I regretted waiting and wanting him to come home so soon.

Fear was constant. The fear of being physically and verbally abused. I couldn't help but wish to be at home with Grandma in Buziaș. It was much better there than here.

I missed Mom. I also missed the greenery and the beautiful flowers everywhere in Buziaș. I felt very sad and lonely on my first day in Bacova because of my conversation with Dad.

I did not know he could be so stubborn. I wanted to stay in Buziaș, where I could run around at the Buziaș Central Park and in the wooden colonnade with my sister and brother.

I continued to remove the grass from the ground to make a dirt path. I couldn't help but feel miserable. Standing in the scorching heat all day, the entire field smelled like dry yellow grass, and many flies constantly harassed me. *There's got to be more to life than this,* I thought as I collected grass into a pile.

I began to think about what it must be like to live in America. A while ago, a kid older than me held a fancy-looking aluminum soda can; he said that the can was made in America. The kid also said he was going to America because they have freedom. Ever since then, I have also dreamt of going to America. I was always fascinated by planes in the sky because I knew those people were possibly going to America.

There seemed to be so much freedom there—much more than what I found here. I am almost six years old and have learned nothing but hard labor. Someday I will go to America and live a free life and not have to suffer here. I know that day will happen. I will make it my mission to make this dream happen. The struggle to find peace in these laborious times is very difficult because I can see my dad complaining about how the government heavily controls the possessions that belong to the peasants. All their work gear, farms, animals, and equipment are taken away and brought to the warehouse for everyone to share. Everyone must be equal. However, I heard that America is the land of opportunity, even from a young age. I can't stop thinking about America.

As I day-dreamt, I turned to my right and saw a truck hauling several men sitting on the truck's bed. I immediately turned my head for a double take. *Those men were holding rifles!* They drove right past us in a hurry somewhere.

"Dad," I screamed and ran to him. I told him about the men with guns; I was extremely terrified. *I wondered where they were going.*

"Never mind that boy! Listen, there is a school a mile away from here. It will be perfect for you and your siblings," Dad reminded me.

"Who will take me there?" I asked.

"It's only a mile. You can walk there." Dad said.

"School will start next week. Until then, I will teach you about hard labor." Dad continued.

"Why does everything have to be about hard labor, Dad? I want to go inside." I was crying.

"In this country, you must work and keep working. That is how it works," he said.

OVERWHELMED

I was unsure what Dad meant by what he said, but ever since he became a communist way before my time, all he knows is hard work.

As a boy, I was observing my dad and my mom's conversations, and I could understand what this country is now becoming—a communist country. As I went about my day, people often mentioned that the government was doing a headcount of everyone who had become a communist. Anyone who was not a communist was not given higher privileges such as good food, cheap rent, gas tanks, work supplies, or land. I did not understand much, but as I got older, I was much more aware of the political events happening in this country.

It seemed strange to me. *Why was Dad working so much every day if he was a communist?* He would be out in the fields from sunrise to sunset, working on his tractor and repairing them. He would not even receive good pay. It was just enough for rent, food, clothes, and some other essentials. We didn't live above our expenses.

THE MOTIVE OF COMMUNISM

After the CAP removed everything from that farm, he became very abusive. The communist government knew that Dad's friend was wealthy, so they took everything. In Romania, everything had to be at the same level. The rich must lose some for the poor to have some.

Dad thought that since he was a communist, he would not have his possessions taken away, but the communists took what he had anyway, making him very mad.

Now, Dad is overworking almost daily because he easily complies with communist orders. Their orders were to overwork and stay busy. What Dad did not know was the Regime's motive was to prevent people from uncovering and talking about the socialist corruption going on around the country. The only way to do that was to overwork the people so they would stay busy and not focus on the corruption. Dad just complied without thinking twice. That was why he always wanted to work. However, it did not make sense to me because now he is leading our family to work more for less. I now assume he was following the productivity-increasing policy that had just been released in the country. However, I did not know that.

Dad was a Secretary Communist in Romania and was respected in the community. This meant that he had the privilege of contributing in high-level meetings with the general secretary of the country. Dad thinks that if he works more and does what the communist leaders tell him, he will gain more respect and privilege. That was why Dad wanted to become a communist in Romania, to gain more privilege.

When the communists give you more privileges, you can do what the peasants cannot do. You will be able to work in most available jobs across Romania. You will have access to fresh foods and not have to wait in line for hours at the store. Still, that will not be enough to travel out of the country. Only the highly respected communist leaders can leave Romania. Everyone else must stay within the Romanian borders. The communists were trying to close our minds by having many people work extra hours.

Prime Minister Gheorghe Gheorghiu-Dej wanted many people to keep on working and only focus on that.

Many suspicions permeated throughout the land, and very few people became aware of what was really happening. Only wise people would understand that the communist party would blind people with extra work, so they would be distracted from what was happening behind the scenes. The Romanian communist party wanted to remain in power and stay strong over the people so they could execute their agenda. Their agenda was to execute common ownership of productivity, the use of money, and for the rich to give all they have to the poor.

Socialism is what is happening all across Romania, as you can see in the State Farm and Cooperativa Apricola De Productie. Again, the CAP is when all possessions are taken from the rich and stored in the State Farm for the peasants and everyone to share.

Even as a six-year-old child, I understood what was happening because Dad and our entire family were given, to some degree, extra privileges. While many other peasants, being poor farmers with low social status, who refused to become part of the Communist Party were not given more privileges. Many wise farmers refused to become communists because they saw the socialism and destruction that followed. They hid their possessions so the Romanian communist officers wouldn't confiscate them.

Few Romanian peasants knew the purpose of communism in Romania, but they did not want to support this party. However, my dad and I were not peasants as I was young, but my dad observed all that was happening to the other poor farmers.

Dad did not realize this truth; he fell for the bait and was given extra privileges for working extra hard every day and becoming part of the party.

I slowly became aware of this truth as I looked around me. I was too young to comprehend all that was happening thoroughly, but as I grew older, I understood what was happening to the farmers due to socialism based on what I was hearing. Many poor farmers who had many possessions are now poor because of socialism.

This affected our family because Dad would become physically abusive if we did not comply with what he wanted, and he wanted us to work every day.

I did not get paid when I went to work with him, but he wanted to teach me that working hard is how I should learn in life. He believed that people who are motivated from a young age would become successful. I did not always believe that hard labor creates motivation, but that is what my dad thought at the time.

I could not stand this any longer, especially after I created a pathway on the grass field and was yelled at by Dad. This was very difficult for me.

I realized I was wrong. I thought I could create a great bond between my dad and me once he returned from the army, but I had a much closer connection with my mom than I did with my dad.

My expectations were still not met. I waited over two years for my dad to come home. It had gotten worse since he came back. I could not withstand this disappointment, especially when I was around him.

I still wanted to love my father because I knew many other people did not have fathers or mothers, so I chose to be content and respect my dad. I understood that some people are in my life for a season, but I knew I was blessed with a dad who still tried to provide for and love us.

It is not always easy to go through the ups and downs of constant disappointments, even from this early age. One thing I can learn from this experience with my dad is not to set my expectations too high because I may be disappointed if my expectations are not met. I decided to be content, continue to love my dad for who he is, and learn to bond with him the best way I could.

I believed I could still have a great time in the new village, even though I was constantly with my dad. I felt safe with my dad because he found a school just a mile down the road for me. As a young boy, I felt excited to meet new friends while I went to school.

The night before my first day of second-grade class, my brother and I wanted to eat some bread and milk because I was starving.

After a very busy day, Dad had just returned from work late. He seemed to appear heated for some reason. He fed me some sausages and cabbage rolls that he had brought from work. Sometimes Dad fed us about three times a day. Other times we would only have breakfast, and that was it for the whole day because Dad and Mom would go out of town for a week. However, sometimes when my parents leave the house, I take care of my siblings. His mentality was to work more than you eat, which was how I had to abide by while living with him.

This evening, a few hours after dinner, I became hungry again. So, my brother and I tried to help ourselves and ate whatever was left in the kitchen.

"What are you two doing?" Dad shouted as he approached us.

"I was hungry, and I need to eat more before walking to school tomorrow," I told him.

"You've already had plenty. Put the food away and head to bed," Dad said as he placed the food away.

"You can only eat when you are hungry, not when you feel like eating, Viorel," Dad continued as he walked into his room.

"Are you saying I can't eat? I don't understand. I am hungry!" I replied with a loud tone.

Dad came out of his room with a belt and rushed toward me. "What did you say? Never talk to me with that tone, son," Dad replied angrily and loudly.

He severely punished my brother and me with a black leather, heavy belt. Mom tried to stop him from hitting us, but he pushed her away so he could discipline us.

"Stefan! What is the reason for this?" Mom shouted.

"These two already ate! Do you want us to run out of food?" he asked her.

"I'll give them something to eat. Go to your room, Stefan. I'll take care of them," Mom said.

Looking at us, Mom said, "Both of you, go to bed. I will make you and your sister a big breakfast tomorrow morning."

"Off to bed, quickly, before I change my mind!" Dad yelled. "This is all your fault, Viorel. Why did you make it so obvious for him?" my brother asked angrily.

"What's wrong with being assertive?" "What's wrong? You cost us our late-night snack! Now we can't eat anymore," my brother complained.

Late that night, my sister asked us what had happened.

"Dad just wants us to starve to death," I told her.

"Well, I saw you eat during dinner. You already ate a lot," my sister said.

"Okay, thanks for taking Dad's side. Just leave us alone," I said. Mom came into our room. "Do not be afraid, Viorel. Your father is going through too much right now. I'll be here with you."

"I can't have one more meal before bed. I do not understand." I replied.

Mom looked at me with confident eyes. "We'll wait for your dad to head off to work, and we will cook some food together. How does that sound?"

I looked at her with a smile. My eyes began to sparkle from tears. Mom kissed my forehead and got up to walk away. As she left, I asked one more question.

"Mom!" I said in a quiet tone.

"Yes, darling?" Mom said as she turned around.

"Did Dad apologize for hitting you in the kitchen last week? I was there, and I saw it happen." I said Curiously.

She smiled at me and said, "I forgave your dad for what he did. That is the most important thing, darling. Forgiveness is for my benefit, and I am happy. Now off to bed!"

That did not answer my question, but her words taught me a valuable lesson for the future. I will never know if Dad asked for forgiveness. Maybe Mom hid that away from me so I would not be hurt.

The next morning, I woke up at about 5 a.m. My brother and I wanted to make breakfast quickly with Mom before Dad woke up. As I cracked my door open, I realized Dad was already up and prepared to leave for Remetea Mare for work. He packed his lunch and his supplies. Then he went outside to check his bicycle tire PSI. Mom also came out and began to heat up some eggs for me.

I came out of my room to eat some food. Dad came back inside and up to me as I was helping Mom prepare breakfast.

"Listen," he said. "I didn't mean to be so hard on you yesterday."

I just stood there and looked at him the whole time he spoke. I did not know what to say; I was intimidated.

"I was stressed with work and didn't mean to put all my anger on you. I apologize," Dad said.

When Dad told me those words, I could not believe it. It confused me because now it seemed he punished me with a leather belt because he had a bad day at work. That seemed somewhat selfish to me, but I could not comprehend it. I felt overwhelmed as a kid when I tried to apologize because I thought he would try to hit me again. I told Vasile about Dad's apology, but we both knew that Dad would do this again.

Mom looked at me and whispered as she was heating up eggs, "Remember what I said about forgiveness last night? It is your medicine. Do not forgive him because he deserves it. Forgive him because you deserve peace."

"Love your father, Viorel. Your dad cares about you. I know he does," Mom said in a loving tone.

After our conversation, Dad left for work on his bicycle, and I headed for my first day of school while my sister and brother stayed home and played with their toys. I deliberately walked at a slow pace so I could process my emotions. My mind was everywhere. I looked up at the sky and observed the clouds and trees. Nature was very therapeutic for me. Then, while pondering what my dad had recently done to me, my eyes began to water up, and my chest began to hurt as I started to cry. I felt like Dad did not care about my first day of school, especially after how he treated me.

Mom's words were very comforting to me. I was so glad to have her at home during this challenging time between my dad and me. I just wished Dad would express his love for my whole family and me in a way I understood.

3

THE HARDSHIP, ROMANIA, 1960

I enjoyed the beautiful sky view on an early Monday morning as I walked to my school; still hurting emotionally, but I was okay. After ten minutes of walking, I turned to my left and could not believe my eyes. Dead horses filled a huge dirt yard. This was in the Cooperativa Apricola De Productie State Farm station, where the communists stored all the confiscated supplies and goods. I saw about one hundred horses of all colors: white, brown, and black, scattered across the dirt, dead. Some of them were cut open and left abandoned. Not one of them was alive.

No one seemed to care. I remember feeling terrified when I saw them. I thought, who could have done such a thing to innocent horses? Fences surrounded the yard's perimeter, so I could not look closer.

What happened? They're not sleeping. I know for a fact. Who killed them all? I thought to myself. My mind tried to process what my eyes had just seen. Then suddenly, my mind flashed back to when I helped my dad out on the fields. I remembered a pickup truck with Romanian communist soldiers sitting on the truck bed, carrying rifles and pistols. They looked at me as they drove off.

Could it be that those men in that pickup truck killed these horses? Maybe they are part of the communist party.

Although the Russian soldiers were heavily present throughout the larger cities of Romania, they weren't often seen in the village. Maybe they caused such devastating deaths to these horses. Maybe it wasn't them.

I was certain the dead horses were confiscated from peasants who owned them. Then they were brought to the yard to be killed for meat.

I was running late for class, but I planned to tell Mom and Dad what I had just seen.

After seeing the dead horses, I felt terrified. What if President Ceausescu orders his soldiers to go from house to house and shoot everyone dead? Fear crept in on me. I was unaware of what had just happened. I did not expect to start my first day feeling terrified, but when I went to class, I spoke to other students about what I had seen in the fields.

I was a bit shy as a little kid. Either way, I tried my best to make friends in class and play games with other students on the playground. I enjoyed being around other kids because I had felt very lonely in the new small village.

Living in this small shabby home was extremely uneventful. Being in class was much better for me than staying at home, where I was alone and sad.

Most days, we had no electricity at my house. We typically used a kerosene-powered lamp to light the room. I tried to hang out with my siblings, but they were all I had.

The food at home was sometimes scarce, but they served good food at school. I realized I would not mind staying there, away from home. I enjoyed the company of friends around me. It made me feel accepted, secure, and happy.

Once class was over, I walked into a first-grade class down the hall to see what other kids at a higher-grade level were doing. Suddenly, from across the room, I saw a gorgeous girl sitting at a desk and working on a drawing.

She immediately caught my attention. She had long, curly, brunette hair. I walked up to her and said, "That is an interesting drawing of clouds and lightning. What is your name?"

"My name is Renica, and these are not clouds and lightning. It is a drawing of a family tree rising to the sky." She replied.

I guess she had not yet colored in the drawing. I could not accurately identify what she was drawing, but the art still looked very impressive.

"What is the meaning of this drawing?" I asked curiously.

"Our family. I drew deep roots in the ground to represent our strength and love. This is our family tree rising to the sky. It is a very tall tree." Renica replied.

"Well, I wish my family was that way. There is always drama between my parents," I mentioned.

"Okay," she replied. Renica went further, "I also sometimes go through hard times within my own family. That is why I drew this art. The teacher asked us to draw something that will help encourage us in hard times so that we will know that happiness is always possible," Renica said and smiled.

"Wow, I wish my class was as fun as yours. All I did was play and talk to random kids in the room," I told her.

"Well, class is about over," Renica said. "I must get going. It was nice talking to you."

The Hardship, Romania, 1960

Renica and I continued to talk much more throughout the year, and we became great friends. I headed home. I hoped Mom had prepared food for my sister, brother, and me.

Later that day, I told my dad about that pickup truck with men on it, but he did not believe me. Maybe he did not see them drive by. They were about twenty yards away, and my dad had his head down, working. He did not pay attention to them.

Dad had been assigned to attend a big work project on the state farm at Remetea Mare, so he had to leave very soon. Mom talked to him about having my aunt stay with us again while he was gone. Mom was going with him, and she did not want us to be alone at home.

"The kids loved her on her last visit when she was here. They will be thrilled to see her again," she told Dad. He said he would talk to my aunt so she could come over before nightfall.

Mom and Dad left before my aunt arrived. Mom left a key under the mat so that my aunt could open the door and prepare some food she said she would buy.

I started walking home from school, and to our surprise, Mom and Dad were not home, but Mom left the house keys under the mat. Dad had left for a short business trip to another town, which he usually goes to about once a month. My mom had gone with him on his business trip to support him. My sister, brother, and I were home alone, and we did not know what to do because there was no dinner prepared for us, and we were famished. The worst part was that there was hardly any power in this house, as was previously mentioned, and it never became better, especially when hard storms hit our area.

I felt compelled to lead the household and care for my sister and brother. I tried my best to find food around the house and fix a small dinner for the three of us. It was not a fancy dinner of any kind. I was able to prepare easy soup meals for them.

I went to the well outside and collected some water. Then I boiled the water on the wood stove. Preparing soup was an easy and fast dish because after you place the noodles in hot boiling water, you only stir a little bit and wait for the food to finish cooking. I found some noodles in the pantry. It only took about fifteen minutes to prepare the delicious soup, and boy was it tasty. My sister and my brother loved how I prepared food. Their comments were thoughtful, which kept me cooking for other people. The type of stove that we used to boil water and heat food was an old pedestal wood stove, gray and clayish in appearance. We used wood to light a spark and create a flame inside the oven. As a very young kid, I tried not to burn myself as I placed food inside the pedestal wood stove. The heat was concentrated and very hot. I remember my sister becoming anxious as I used the wood stove because usually, Mom and Grandma knew best how to use it.

Since the water was not working in the house, my brother and I went to collect some from the outside well. This was our main water source at the time, and we needed to use this water for cooking, bathing, and drinking. We had taken just enough water each day while Mom and Dad were away from home, so we were very thankful.

The water shut off the night before Mom and Dad had left, and my brother constantly complained about us not having our water supply. He preferred to have plenty of water while bathing, and this tragedy was a huge concern for him.

My sister and I held the house together while our parents were away, but I was considered the man of the house. Whenever my brother or my sister needed help in any way, I always jumped to help. I cared about my brother and sister, so I did my best to help.

The Hardship, Romania, 1960

I gathered more water from the well outside and placed the water in the shower base for my brother so he could bathe. Bathing these days was not convenient. We used a single flat base. You would stand on the flat base and use your hands or a bucket to cover yourself with water.

We heated the water lightly in the wooden stove during the winter and used warm or hot water for bathing that way too. When the power and water turned off, the three of us lived like those people during the Middle Ages. Although we found ourselves in a difficult time, we remained content because the three of us supported each other.

When it got dark outside, we became hungry and struggled to find food. We decided to take a nap and hoped our parents would arrive soon.

It was common for us to get hungry while living with Dad because when he left for his business trips, he was typically gone for two to three days. It was not safe for my sister, brother, and me to be alone at home for that long without supervision.

We were terrified of the dark, waiting for Mom to arrive home from work. We heard strange humming and wind noises from outside. The walls cracked every so often.

Mom had just arrived home earlier than Dad. He was still finishing some things up. She was very excited to see us. She always smiled when she came home from work because she wanted to be hospitable and care for us

Mom asked as she hung her hat and bag up on the hangers, "How was everything while I was gone, kids?" She immediately knew something was wrong because she expected to see four pairs of shoes near the front door, but there were only three.

"Well, it was horrible, Mom, that is all I have to say," I expressed with a careless tone.

Mom hurried to put her things away as she talked to us. It felt like no one cared about us anymore. We were left at home alone for almost a day, and we were fed up with being left alone at home.

Mom laughed a bit, "Hey, if your aunt didn't give you guys enough chocolate when she arrived, then we can find someone else to watch over you three."

I interrupted, "I know you and Dad both have jobs to go to, so you leave us all alone with no food, water, or lights. I had an attitude as I walked away.

"What?!" Mom screamed as she ran about the house looking to find her."

Do you mean to tell me she was not here to watch over you three while I was gone?" Mom said with disappointment on her face.

"She was supposed to be here?" I asked. "No, we were here, alone, with no food, water, or lights this whole time!"

"Wait! Wait! What is going on?" my sister shouted.

"I cannot believe this," Mom said. "I told Dad to have her stay with you guys while we were away."

"No, Mom, we were here alone, starving. All we had was water from the well outside to drink. By the way, most of these petroleum lamps are all used up. Will the lights turn back on? It has been about two days with no lights," my sister tried to explain.

"I do not know," Mom said. "We will wait until Dad returns home in a few hours," as she rushed to prepare food.

"Woah! By the way, Mom! On my way to School two days ago, I saw hundreds of dead horses scattered across the field next to our campus," I said. "A week ago, I saw a truck pass by with men holding rifles and guns. They drove off. Maybe they killed the horses, Mom!" I insisted.

The Hardship, Romania, 1960

"You do not need to worry about that," she told me uneasily. "Just eat your food and wait for Dad to come home."

Mom served our food. She was in a hurry, and I could tell she was frustrated at Dad for misunderstanding.

Mom was very concerned for us as well. She made sure we were okay, healthy, and safe. All of us in the room were very confused about what happened because we did not know that my aunt was supposed to stay with us while Mom and Dad were gone.

Although we had a terrible experience the past few days, I was used to it. This was not the first time it had happened. Sleeping hungry and thirsty was normal for us. Sometimes when my parents were out for a few days, Mom and Dad would plan to have a family friend watch over us, but other times they left and put me in charge of the house. This can be beneficial. Since I have overseen the house, I often had to learn how to prepare food for my siblings and myself. I had no choice but to place myself in a position of high responsibility.

I became street-smart as I tried my best to survive while my parents were gone out of town. While I was alone at home, it was all about survival and trying not to sleep on an empty stomach. I did not think anything would improve, especially with this country under communist power.

Dad made it home from work, and immediately a loud commotion started in my home. Mom tried to understand what was happening in Dad's head because he apparently left us alone at home, but Dad paid no attention to her. Instead, he showed her the horse meat he brought home from work. His supervisor offered him an unusually large portion of horse meat for our family.

Not many people received this amount of horse meat unless they were a communist. Dad knew this meat was taken from the horses that had previously been killed, but I did not realize it then. I was only happy to eat the meat that he brought home. However, Dad told Mom it was beef. He told her that so she would eat it and allow us to eat it. Everyone can be full and satisfied.

Mom immediately remembered what I had told her about the dead horses out in the field. She had a disgusted look on her face as she backed away from Dad, still holding the horse meat. She then knew he had lied to her and deceived her. She was disappointed and began to lose trust in him.

"Kids, go in the room now!" she demanded.

It was getting dark outside, and the lights still did not work in our home, so the entire house was mostly dark, despite the lamps. Mom went into her room with Dad and shut the door behind them. Then they argued for about an hour about why Dad left us alone at home. The walls gave no privacy for their loud conversation. It seemed as if Dad was careless because he was concerned more about his possessions and performance at work as a mechanic. He hardly paid attention to Mom as she constantly called out to him. It was as if she was talking to a cold brick wall. Mom cared so much for our family, and she could not cope with Dad prioritizing his job over our family. The argument continued with Dad yelling and talking back to Mom in anger.

My sister, brother, and I were in the kitchen trying to sleep, but we were distracted by the constant commotion coming from my parent's room. We were eager to eavesdrop on their conversation.

I was fed up with them arguing every day. Why can't there be peace in our home? We did not understand what was going on. As we were eavesdropping on their conversation, the three of us began to talk about what we were hearing. Suddenly, we heard a loud bang coming from my parent's room. We were freaking out because we did not know what was going on. It turned out that Dad hit the wall in anger.

"Do you know what Viorel told me today? Mom said with frustration. Mom continued, "On his way to school two days ago, he saw a yard full of dead horses. And here you are, coming home with what, horse meat?" Mom challenged.

Dad stood silent for a few seconds, then said, "This is beef. What are you talking about?"

"Oh, okay, beef? That is not very convincing. What did I just tell you? Viorel saw dead horses out in the CAP yard! You're still lying to me?

What? Do you want to starve again like you did while I was away in the military?" Dad asked.

"I would much rather go through that again than for you to constantly lie to me. You need to stop," Mom said with concern in her voice.

"Those horses were ordered to be shot and killed by the communist leaders. Do you want the kids to know all about this? I don't want this horse meat. Take it back. I do not want our kids to see what is happening out there. We will not support the mass murder of horses and then eat them. We can find other food around here," Mom said again.

"Do you want to starve? Huh? My supervisor gave me an unusual portion of horse meat for our family. It tastes just like beef. The kids will not realize that it is horse meat!" Dad yelled.

"You're out of your mind!" Mom replied. "I am not supporting this; I will not. Viorel already saw the dead horses. I do not want him and the kids to know what they are eating. Just take it back," Mom shouted, and she began to cry.

"If we do not accept extra portions of horse meat from my supervisor, they will think that we are rich. We will no longer receive other privileges like other fellow communists," Dad continued. We could hear the rage rising in Dad's voice.

"I care more about our kids. I do not want to feed them murdered horses," Mom insisted.

"Woman! I will keep bringing this meat home, and you will do as I say," Dad demanded, and he began physically abusing her.

The three of us ran to their door and tried open it to stop Dad from hurting her, but we were unable to get the door open.

"Open the door!" my sister shouted with tears in her eyes. She held the doorknob with both hands.

The atmosphere began to feel very dark and disturbing as we tried to stop Dad from hitting Mom. I heard slapping noises coming from the room for over a minute. Rodica wasn't able to open the door. She heard more slapping and footsteps and Mom crying. Then Mom busted the door open, and my sister fell to the floor. Mom tried to get away from my dad. She ran outside crying loudly.

"What have you done?" I asked Dad.

"Run for cover! We must get out of here!" my sister yelled and ran towards me. Dad distanced himself from everyone.

Several months went by, and our family affairs de-escalated. Dad became calmer, but I was afraid to spend time with him because I never knew how he might act toward me.

Instead, I approached my mom as she was reading the Bible on the couch. We were alone. My sister and brother were in the kitchen, and Dad was outside working on a tractor.

"Mom?" I said.

"Yes, Vio, come here, gorgeous," she replied.

"I already asked you this last time, but how are you feeling? Dad is being very mean to you," I asked. I had always been a momma's boy and wanted her to be safe.

"I'm doing great, Vio. Don't worry. Dad and I are working everything out. It's okay," she said.

"Oh, I know how you two communicated in that room. He hit you, and I saw you running out the door, crying," I said sarcastically.

Mom knew that I had become acquainted with their affairs, and she did not want the aspects of that to negatively impact me. There was really nothing she could do because Dad acts out randomly throughout the day if something is not going in his favor.

I began to cry, sitting next to her. She means the world to me. I hate to see physical violence happening to Mom. She doesn't deserve hardship.

"Mom, please tell me everything will be okay. I'm scared of Dad. I don't know what to do." I held onto her arm and looked at her with tears dripping down my cheeks.

"Aww, sweetie, how about we read through this chapter together?" asked Mom asked quietly. I developed sinus pressure and a runny nose, and my throat became tense from crying.

"Okay, Mom, I love you, Mom, I love you, I said to her through sniffles."

Then we read together through Psalms 33. It talks about how fitting it is for the godly to praise the Lord and to sing for joy. We continued to read through this chapter, and we started an interesting conversation about God and the different parts of the Bible. It was quite liberating.

After about an hour of discussion, we both felt the atmosphere shift into a much lighter setting. We felt joy and a sense of peace that we'd never experienced before. I forgot why I was even crying.

It was hilarious because I asked Mom why I was crying an hour ago, and she said, "I don't know. You tell me."

I said, "I can't remember," and we just looked at each other for a second and laughed.

This experience was something I had never experienced with any other book. There is something powerful about the Holy Bible. I did not know what it was, but it definitely has some power when two people share it.

Then about three weeks later, I told my mom I wanted to spend time with Dad when he got back from work. Part of me did not want to because only God knows how Dad will act, especially after work. But Mom insisted I go out and play with my brother in the street instead. My brother was consistently hyper, and he needed someone to play with.

I took my brother with me out on the street around noon time. The street was not too wide, with ditches on either side. I carried a ball with me. My brother and I bounced the ball back and forth and played catch during the hot July weather. The ball was a basketball-sized ball, red and bouncy. I became very annoyed with my brother because he would return the ball at a breakneck speed when I passed the ball to him. He continued to do that for about ten minutes. I told him to stop throwing the ball too fast, but he would just laugh and carelessly throw at fast speeds toward me.

So, in my anger, I walked alongside the street and picked up a small rock about the size of a golf ball. Then, as my brother was still laughing, I threw the rock at him. The rock hit his head, and he fell hard onto the hot, dirty, unforgiving asphalt.

His head began to bleed, and he started crying loudly. As my brother lay on the ground, he placed his hand on his head to feel what had happened, and then he saw blood on his fingers and started to cry even more.

The Hardship, Romania, 1960

"Calm down. You're not so tough now, are you?" I said to my brother. Then I saw Mom rushing out of the house. She had seen everything through the window.

"Viorel, why did you hurt your brother? Get inside! We will discuss this in the house!" Mom yelled.

I became terrified because I knew what awaited me inside that house—a black leather belt and a lot of pain and screaming behind locked doors. I decided to run off down the street to get away from Mom and escape the punishment. I kept on running, thinking I had gotten away from my mom, but I was wrong. Mom girded up her long skirt and chased after me. She snapped off a branch from a tree and chased after me with it.

As Mom and I ran down the long street, neighbors came out of their houses to investigate the commotion. Some cheered me on, saying, "Come on! Save yourself; keep running!"

"Get back here, Viorel. You are in big trouble, mister!" Mom yelled angrily.

Suddenly, this big kid ran up to me, caught me, held both of my arms, and yelled out, "Here he is. I got him for you," he said, laughing.

"Let me go!" I shouted. I was panting. I tried to fight this kid off, but his grip was tight. Then, as soon as Mom caught up to us, the kid let go, and I ran off again.

"You got this, buddy. Don't let her catch you. Save yourself!" the kid yelled after he set me free.

"Stop right now! Viorel or I am going to tell Dad. You will be punished severely for this!" Mom shouted, trying to catch her breath. I kept running. A man with his children beside him stood outside their home, cheering me on. The man shouted, "Turn right into the nearest old white carpentry shop." So, I turned and went inside to hide from my mom.

My hands were shaking. I locked the door in fear. I took a few steps back and began to cry. I looked outside through the old, dirty window inside the shop.

I saw Mom walking around the outer perimeter of the shop, trying to find me. She looked lost, holding the tree branch in her right hand. Then suddenly, she saw me through the window, and with an angry face, she said, "There you are. Just wait until I get my hands on you, Viorel. I am not finished with you! When you get home, you will get a painful spanking!" Then Mom stepped away from the window and walked home.

I did not understand why Mom was so concerned about what I had done. The entire time, my brother was still on the ground crying, and Mom only cared about punishing me. I was afraid for my life. I thought it was all over. I was trapped and did not know where else to go from there.

Then, I realized Mom was trying to gain access to the other side of the building. He had to pass through a garden to get to the other side of the building. She approached a big tree in the garden that had a giant beehive embedded in it. The bees became my allies. The swarm of bees formed a large, thick cloud and buzzed over Mom. I watched as Mom immediately dropped her tree branch and took off running. I was so happy that the bees chased her away. I just knew I had escaped from punishment.

As Mom ran off screaming and violently waving her arms, people stood outside, wondering what was happening. When they realized what had happened, they began to laugh. I started brainstorming how I should return home. Maybe I needed to wait two hours or so to give Mom's anger time to die down. Then, hopefully, I would not be punished so severely.

I quickly ran out of the building to the nearest house to hide. I knocked on their door. A man answered the door and immediately perceived something terrible had happened to me. I was shaking. My face was red from the tears running down my face. I told him what had happened, and he let me into his home to rest for a short time.

It began to get dark outside. The man and his wife offered to take me with their two kids to harvest hay for their cows. They told me I was safe. They encouraged me by telling me my mom would not hurt me anymore.

I enjoyed the field tour as I walked around in the dark, holding my flashlight. It was not too dark outside because the full moon was very bright. That night we could see parts of the field in the dark.

Suddenly, I looked down and saw what looked like a rabbit just a few feet away from where I was standing. The rabbit did not move. It was utterly still. It did not seem afraid at all. It looked so cute. I approached the rabbit to take a closer look. I held my palms together to try to pick it up. I caught it and held it in my hands. The rabbit did not resist at all. It was fascinating. I immediately thought, wait until Mom sees what I caught. If she sees I have a pet, then she won't punish me as severely because the rabbit will witness it.

I walked off slowly to see if Mom was outside looking for me, but she wasn't. A couple of hours later, the man said I should go home where I belonged, but his wife insisted I come inside their home and stay for a little longer, so I went inside.

I sat down to have dinner with this amazing, wealthy family. As we ate, I shared a bit more about why my mom became angry, and they felt so sorry for me.

After dinner, the family decided to escort me home so I wouldn't be alone and afraid in the dark.

When I approached the house, I opened the door, and the people I had stayed with told Mom not to hurt me. They told her I was a good kid.

By now, my mother had treated my brother's injury. I showed Mom the new pet I found. Mom decided not to punish me. I became so thankful that the bees rescued me from great punishment. The whole day was just chaotic.

I was a bit upset because my brother had exaggerated his injury. I know he was bleeding from the head, but he didn't need to create a huge scene for Mom to find out what had happened. Eventually, we got over it.

A couple of weeks later, my grandma came from Buziaș to visit us. When I saw her for the first time in months, I ran to her and gave her a big hug. She brought fresh milk and almond chocolate. I was satisfied. We began to talk and spend time together. She also prepared some fresh cabbage rolls, which I won't deny.

Grandma always made the best cabbage rolls. They consisted of several delicious ingredients: ground pork, long-grain rice, onions, fresh parsley, bacon, tomato juice, and so much more.

Rodina, Vasile, and I gathered in the kitchen to see Grandma cook it up. The fresh smell of the cabbage rolls permeated the entire house, and my stomach began to growl. We enjoyed the food and had a great time spending time with Grandma.

She is definitely funny. Grandma always finds a way to make us laugh, even when she is not trying. She had the best jokes to tell us at the most random times. One joke she shared went like this: If a man is getting baptized but has no faith, he will only get wet. That is very true because that man is better off taking a shower.

Grandma's visit refreshed me after some hard days with Dad. It was a great time to laugh again after such a long time. Later, Grandma mentioned that her visit would take one of us back to Buziaș with her. I wanted to go back with her, but I also wanted to stay in Bacova with my mom. It was a dilemma for me. However, I made my choice to stay with Mom.

I told Grandma to take my brother. He was too hyper and causing trouble. I wanted to get rid of him because I couldn't stand his constant outrageous behavior. My sister wanted to stay with me. My brother agreed to return to Buziaș because he wanted to get away from my dad.

Grandma needed one of us because Zoia was alone at her house. She needed someone to play with. Zoia was still grieving her grandpa's death, and it was hard for her to be alone at home. Since my brother is hyper and very active, I thought he could play with Zoia out in the fields.

Grandma and my brother then headed back to Buziaș two days later.

After my brother had left, the house became so much quieter. I thought, maybe when my brother plays with Zoia in the fields of Buziaș, he can learn how to catch a rock. I decided I was a little rough on my brother this past week. He was upset with me after what I did to him. Overall, I still loved him as a brother. Sometimes I caught myself taking my humor too far, and I ended up causing trouble as a result.

Early the next morning, I went to school on foot, and about midway, I heard a loud scream coming from the house to my right. The constant commotion from the house disturbed me. I saw a crowd of armed men in uniform walking into the house. A woman's voice begged them not to take her animals from her yard. The men had intruded on the woman's home and wanted to take her pigs and chickens away.

I slowly approached the house to eavesdrop on the conversation quietly. The woman began to scream, "NO!" Then I heard multiple gunshots blasting across the street. The sound waves in the air from those gunshots pounded my chest violently. I involuntarily jumped, filled with a sudden fight-or-flight response.

I quickly turned and ran in fear, thinking I would be the next one to get shot. I ran all the way to school. My body flooded with adrenaline. I was scared for my life; I did not want to be next.

When I made it to the School, I suddenly stopped running. I stooped down and laid my hand on a pillar, trying to catch my breath.

My friend, Renica, came up to me and said with a concerned look, "School doesn't start for another thirty minutes. You do know that, right?"

I shot Renica a double take. "You won't believe what I just heard," I said, trying to catch my breath.

"What? The school bells? Are you okay, Viorel? You do not look okay," Renica said with concern.

I was breathing heavily while trying to regain my composure to explain better. "I heard someone get shot. I think some lady died. Soldiers were inside her house, and they killed the lady!"

"Just now?"

"It happened five minutes ago on my way to school. I ran all the way here so I would not get shot!" I replied.

"I think my mom told me about that," Renica said. "Soldiers go to rich people's houses and demand their animals."

"Oh no! They're taking their animals for meat again!" I remembered it aloud. "That doesn't make sense. Are they killing those who refuse to comply with the soldier's orders?" I asked her.

"That's what my mom said, yes," Renica confirmed. "I don't think that lady was a communist because she had everything she wanted. My dad lives around here. Many people here are rich," Renica continued.

"Why did she get invaded by those soldiers?" I asked.

"Because of socialism, the communist leaders are influenced by Russia. They take from the rich and give to the poor so that everyone can be even and the same. They confiscated many possessions from castles, homes, and farms where the rich people lived. Most castles are closed, and no one can enter them," Renica shared.

"That is not fair! The rich work so hard to earn their living." I replied angrily.

"I won't disagree with you. We are living in unfair times right now," she said.

"Well, that makes perfect sense because last week, on my way to School, I saw hundreds of dead horses scattered across the main field of Bacova."

"Yes, that land belonged to a rich man," Renica said. "President Gheorghe ordered that they be killed and taken in for meat to feed the poor communists all around Romania."

"I know who killed those horses," I said. "It was a group of communists driving a pickup truck holding rifles in their hands. My dad brought home some meat, lied to my mom, and said it was beef."

I continued to discuss my frustrations. "I can't believe the President would request such horrible destruction in our country. I wish I could leave this country and escape this terrible place," I said.

"Good luck. Only a few highly selected communist leaders who work for Gheorghe can leave this country," Renica informed me.

"I made a promise that someday I will leave this country and fly on a plane to America, the land of the free," I replied, as I began to ponder and stare into the sky.

Renica chuckled, "What makes you believe that?"

"We have no life here. The only way to live is to leave this place," I said.

"Yeah, well, keep dreaming. You cannot make yourself a highly influential communist leader to leave this country." Renica scoffed.

"That is not what I mean. Someday I will leave legally without being a communist leader," I corrected her.

School began, but I could not stop thinking about how bad the government was. That was my ultimate dream ever since I was little. Trouble started as early in my life as I can remember. I believed there was nothing to live for there. Even as a child, I would never dare to start a new family living in Romania. The only place to start a new life is outside of this country since experiencing what communism does to families and businesses. All around me, I saw fear, hunger, and poverty.

Dad told me that Romania used to be a capitalist country. Individuals were allowed to own and control the products in their businesses. Now, because of Russia, Romanian President, Gheorghe Dej, ordered that the regime in this country is to work even harder for the same pay rate. He wanted everyone to become a communist so that everyone would comply with his orders. I believe the President wanted everyone to work hard for less pay so that the people could stop thinking and planning a way out to escape. This was known as the productivity-increasing policy, in which many worked more frequently. As a child, fleeing to America may have seemed like a dream, but I grew more confident that someday it would become my reality. I did not want my future family to live under communist orders. I desperately wanted freedom.

After school, I invited Renica to come over so she, my sister, and I could play the husband-and-wife role-play together. We played this game for fun outside of school because we wanted to pretend we were older and responsible. Renica played the wife, and I played the husband; my sister was the child in the role-play. We usually played this innocent husband and wife role-play occasionally. It was our fun activity after we got home from school as little children. Then after that role-play, the three of us decided to play catch outside on the street during the late evening.

It was a way to get my mind off the stress of where this country was heading. We played catch with a red ball I found in the ditch. It still had plenty of air in the bouncy ball, and we also played tag. The sky grew dark as the sun was setting.

Later, we decided to play soccer out on the street. Renica, my sister, and a few other school friends also came to play. I was the goalkeeper because I have always loved defense. The others were out in the street playing as midfielders. My sister, being my defender, tried her best to manage the ball, but Renica quickly went past her and proceeded in my direction, and ran with the ball. Renica then came sprinting toward me to strike a goal. Something unusual happened as she approached me and attempted to kick the ball past me.

Suddenly, I saw a flash of perfect white light in the sky.

"GOOAAL!" Renica yelled victoriously. Renica began running around with excitement because she had made her first score in the game. I was still on the ground, trying to make sense of what I had just seen. It was nighttime, but a light came out of nowhere for some reason.

Renica and my sister realized I was still on the ground.

"What happened, Viorel?" You were supposed to stop the ball! My sister yelled while trying to catch her breath. My sister was always a bit competitive whenever we played soccer. She didn't like to lose. I am incredibly competitive in the sport of soccer as well, but this bright light threw me off course.

"It seems like I am better than you at this sport," Renica said as she picked me up off the street.

"The ball didn't even hit you," Renica laughed. "Why did you fall down?"

I told Renica and my sister what I had seen. Completely overwhelmed, I was shaking a little.

"I saw something bright in the sky, and I mean extremely bright. I lost my orientation, and then I fell," I replied with a sense of urgency.

"Viorel, it's nighttime. The sun is down," my sister said, confused.

It wasn't the sun. It was something else. My parents put up artificial lights for us to see in the dark as the sun came down, but this other light was different. I explained that we had a white table appear in the sky, and I also saw two white-clothed men standing on either side of the table.

My friends looked at me with concern as I spoke. None of them believed me because I was the only one who saw this.

"I don't know what this means. I think it was a vision. Those two men were talking," I said.

"Were they talking about how bad you were at soccer?" my sister scoffed.

"Enough!" Renica said.

"So, this just happened?" Renica inquired.

"Maybe it was a vision or something," I confessed that it looked so real, and I saw it in the sky.

Renica cared about me. She began to ask more questions about what exactly I had seen. Perhaps this was a message that something might happen to me in the future. I could not hear what the two white-clothed men were talking about. I only saw them for two or three seconds.

Mom came out of the house to see what the commotion was about. So, I explained everything I had just seen in my vision. When I told her I saw a bright white table in the sky with two white-clothed men standing on either side, she looked mesmerized. She believed me, unlike my sister and my other friends.

Mom wondered if I knew what the two men were talking about, but I did not hear anything. I only saw what was happening, and that was all. Then Mom told me not to take this lightly. She said to write it all down in a notebook and save it for later in life. I took her advice. Renica and my other friends from School went home. It was extremely late.

I do not know what this vision meant. I was unsure if it spoke of a future event in my life or if I was going crazy and delusional. All I knew was this had never happened to me before, and it was an overwhelming experience.

The following day was the start of the weekend. Dad and Mom argued about our lack of food in the house. I had not been well-fed recently. I was starving; my entire family was starving.

Dad had enough money to pay the bills, but we did not have enough money to feed the family. The electricity in the house was still not working. We had terrible airflow in the house, and we still did not have enough water to bathe. Dad went out in the backyard to work on the well and tried to get more water for us, but it was a struggle.

Amid our chaos and despair, Grandma arrived at our house along with my brother. Grandma had mentioned that she had lost her tolerance for my brother, he was too hyper, and she couldn't stand him any longer. "Please, take him back!" she demanded.

My brother had a negative attitude when he arrived because he did not want to return to living with Dad again. Grandma wanted my brother to play with his aunt, Zoia, at her home, but he only caused problems and broke things.

"It has only been two weeks!" Mom said with concern. With disappointment, Mom turned to my brother and said, "Is this how you behave at your grandma's house? She is taking care of you, for heaven's sake!"

My brother went into the house. He was disciplined for how he had behaved at Grandma's house. Shortly after, Grandma requested that I come and stay with her at her home and keep Zoia company.

I wanted to move back to Buziaș, but I also wanted to remain with my dad so that I could attend school. I knew I would miss my friends, especially Renica, and I did not want to leave them. If I left, I would have to switch schools and attend another school in Buziaș. My grandma said everything would be okay. She assured me I would make new friends and visit this place to see my old friends again. Besides, Grandma has a pension from the government, and she will cook good food for me. So, I decided to move back to Buziaș with Grandma. At least I can get away from Dad and his negative, abusive behavior.

Grandma and I headed back to Buziaș, I saw my aunt Zoia in the house, and we began to spend time together playing out in the yard. We had a wonderful time, and everything seemed okay, until my first night at Grandma's house. I went to bed but could not sleep because I had experienced bad dreams. I woke up every hour from nightmares, shaking severely. I also had some sort of intense shock sensation in my brain and began to toss and turn for hours during the night. I became terrified in my dream.

The Hardship, Romania, 1960

Grandma woke up because of the moaning sounds I was making. She came running to my room to see what was going on with me.

When Grandma entered my room, she saw foam coming out of my mouth and nose. I was shaking uncontrollably. Grandma asked me what had happened, but I did not know how to respond. I told her my entire body was shaking, and I could not sleep from bad dreams and the electric shock in my brain. She took me out in the backyard and poured water over me to wake me up.

"Did you eat before bed, Viorel?" Grandma asked. She thought maybe I took medication before bed on an empty stomach. She became overly concerned. I started crying because I did not know what was happening to me. I struggled to speak. I tried my best to talk to Grandma and explain how I felt, but it was exceedingly difficult.

I was disoriented as Grandma tried to help me walk back into her house. She rushed me to the hospital for immediate medical attention. As soon as I arrived at the hospital, the pain started to go away. The doctors examined me but did not see anything wrong with me. They said that I was perfectly fine and that maybe it was some sort of allergic reaction.

Grandma knew that I was not allergic to anything. She insisted that they needed to find out what had happened to me. This was not normal. Still, they checked me over a second time and did not find anything wrong.

When the doctors could not find anything the second time, Grandma knew this was a demonic attack against me. My Grandma was an Orthodox Christian. She knew an Orthodox Priest who would help diagnose the problem.

The very next morning, she took me to see Forga, the Orthodox Priest. He told Grandma to come inside the church office, just the two of them. I waited in the sanctuary until they finished discussing some things.

"What clothes does Viorel sleep in every night?" the Orthodox Priest asked.

"He has his favorite pajamas that he puts on before bed. In fact, he slept in them last night, and that's when it all happened," Grandma replied.

"Okay, tomorrow, bring me his favorite pajamas, and I will anoint them with oil in Jesus' Name," the priest instructed.

"Okay, thank you!" Grandma said.

"I think the devil is trying to attack your grandson, Grandma." the priest said. Grandma was immediately terrified by the priest's words.

"How can that be," she asked?

"Do not worry. I will anoint Viorel and his pajamas tomorrow when you arrive. Have a blessed day," said the priest.

As we walked home, I asked my grandma what had happened. She told me everything would be okay and that we would see the priest again tomorrow so he could anoint me. Grandma never told me that the priest would also anoint my pajamas. She kept it a secret and didn't tell me about the anointing.

Back home, Grandma tried to calm me down because I was terrified from last night.

Zoia heard everything that had happened the previous night. "Viorel?" she asked with worry in her voice. "What was going on during the night?"

"I am being attacked at night. I am unable to breathe and stop shaking," I told her. Zoia thought she might be able to diagnose his problem.

"Maybe it is because of the heavy load of anxiety that you carry from your father."

"How could that be?" I asked.

"Well, ever since my father died not too long ago, I haven't been unable to sleep."

"Zoia, you have been through a tough time, but I think I am experiencing something demonic and powerful," I said.

"Hasn't your father, Stefan, inflicted pain into your life? Maybe I can help you." Zoia said.

"Sometimes he does, but Mom comforts me and speaks words of encouragement over me," I shared. "But I will not refuse your help. Thank you for supporting me."

"So why are you going through this at night then?" Zoia asked.

"I am not sure. I am having visions lately, too. Maybe something is about to happen to me." I replied.

I continued to discuss the significant events in my life because she seemed interested. After that, I played catch outside with Zoia to get my mind off the negative things happening to me.

As nighttime approached, Grandma tucked me in bed and began to tell me stories to help me fall asleep. I was very happy she was with me to help me fall asleep because I was afraid to sleep. I did not want to have nightmares again.

When I fell asleep, Grandma left the room. Hours later, while sleeping, I suddenly had a hard time breathing. It felt like someone was choking me with two hands, and I could not move. I began shaking again, and this time, it was twice as bad. For about ten or twenty seconds, I couldn't breathe. I woke up, and the choking sensation was worse. I tried my best to grab the table lamp on the desk beside my bed. Reaching it, I threw it on the ground to get Grandma or Zoia's attention. A few moments later, Grandma came into my room and was terrified for me.

"What happened?" She screamed. Grandma removed my blanket and held me tightly. She encouraged me, telling me that everything would be alright.

Immediately, I was able to breathe again. Panting, I laid sideways on the bed, "It's happening again. I was not able to breathe!" I cried.

Viorel, if this happens again, scream out the name of Jesus, okay? Grandma instructed.

I was not too sure who Jesus was. If this name, Jesus, really helped me sleep, I would always use it to protect myself from nightmares.

Grandma helped me get out of bed. I was so afraid; I was unable to stop crying.

"Is this how I will end up sleeping for the rest of my life?" I asked.

"No! This ends today!" Grandma assured me. It was early in the morning. Darkness still covered the sky. The sun had not yet risen. Grandma held my hand as we walked across town to see the priest. I cried the whole way because I was so traumatized in my sleep when I was unable to breathe.

Grandma and I stopped walking for a second. She knelt to my level and looked at me. What's making you cry, Viorel?

"I can't stop shaking, and it is very dark out here," I confessed.

"Listen, the sun will rise very soon, and we will have light. Everything will be fine. You are safe with me," Grandma assured me in a loving tone.

"Let's go; we are almost there," she said.

The dark sky reminded me of when I was sleeping. I was also afraid of the dark, gritty alley between the houses and small buildings as we walked to meet the priest. I was terrified the whole way, but Grandma was by my side to comfort me.

When we finally arrived to meet the priest, he was already awake and available to meet us. Grandma told me to sit at a distance as she went to discuss some things with him. I did not know it then, but Grandma gave the priest my baby blue pajamas to anoint and pray over. She told the priest everything that had happened, including when the second nightmare attack occurred. She was fed up with all this demonic activity.

The priest asked if this had happened before. Grandma told him it all started happening as soon as I moved back to Buziaș.

"Please help my little grandson. He is a good kid, and he does not deserve this." Grandma pleaded.

After the priest handed my pajamas back to Grandma, she told me to go and meet with the priest. He prayed over me in the name of Jesus and anointed me with oil. The priest said that anointing means smearing oil over someone's forehead or body to receive healing from God when accompanied by faith, as it is taught in scripture (James 5:14).

I did not feel any different after the prayer and anointing. However, I stopped crying because I felt a sudden sense of peace. Grandma was amazed.

The priest had a Bible to pray verses over me, but this was the only Bible he had because the communist regime prohibited them. Grandma was very thankful that he had at least one Bible. He said we were welcome to come again if we needed anything else. Grandma was happy that I had finally received prayer. We walked outside, and the sun was rising. It began to light up the sky with many beautiful colors, and the clouds reflected the redness of the sunrise.

"See, I told you the sun would rise sooner than you thought," Grandma said.

"The sky is amazing, Grandma, and I am not shaking anymore," I said.

"That is great! Let's go home and prepare some good food. What do you say?" Grandma suggested.

When we arrived, Grandma prepared some tasty Romanian food, such as cabbage rolls and bread with sour cream. Zoia and I played catch out on the street. Grandma was very thankful that everything was okay. She had faith that I would no longer be attacked at night.

Once nighttime arrived, Grandma, Zoia, and I gathered for storytime. She spoke about many different historical events that had happened. She would also make up stories. Sometimes during story times before bed, she would make us solve riddles. We had a great time together, and nothing was better than spending time with people I love and those who care for me.

Once it was time for me to go to bed, I put on my pajamas that the priest prayed over, and I went to bed. Grandma tucked me in and kissed my forehead goodnight as I closed my eyes. For some reason, I had forgotten about my past nightmares the last two days. Those memories never came to my mind as I slowly fell asleep. I slept peacefully during the night, and I never woke up during the night. I did not have nightmares or shaking sensations.

I woke up the next morning, stretched, and let out a big yawn. I walked to the kitchen to be with Grandma and spent time with her that morning. I spent the first few hours of my day not realizing the restful sleep I had last night. Grandma had asked me if I slept okay. I suddenly jumped with excitement because I did not realize I had slept peacefully. I completely forgot. I was totally amazed and thankful that, for once, I was able to rest in peace.

I could not express the joy and love in the room. The entire house was filled with a new atmosphere and felt very refreshing.

The Hardship, Romania, 1960

Afterward, Grandma told me that Forga, the priest, prayed over my pajamas, which was why I never struggled through the night.

It was hard to believe because I did not know he did this for me. Also, I knew that there must be a God out there because even the doctors could not solve this problem I was having. Only a simple prayer healed and fixed the entire situation. I became very thankful and joyful for the rest of that week because I never had a nightmare again.

A NEW ERA, 1965

Years passed since I left my grandma in Buziaș. At the age of twelve, I lived with my father and mother again. While I stayed in Buziaș, my parents relocated to another village which is twenty-five kilometers east of Timișoara. There, you will only find breathtaking agriculture. There are dozens of mulberry trees, plum trees, and apple trees that scatter the fields.

Nothing much had changed with Dad. He was still the hard-working man that he was. Despite the challenging living conditions from being under my father's roof, the country experienced substantial relief for the past seven years.

Since 1944, the Soviet military occupation of Romania has been frightening to many people, especially the rich. The Soviet Union maintained a heavy military presence throughout the entire land, causing violence and damage to many properties. Romania soon became a satellite of the Union of Soviet Socialist Republics in 1948.

Thanks to President Gheorghe Gheorghiu-Dej, who also was the first communist leader of Romania in 1947, they removed the Soviet military presence from the country on July 25, 1958. My entire family received the great news that day over the radio Bucharest announcement. That day was the biggest celebration. At last, the 14 years of heavy micro-management of the 35,000 Russian troops roaming our country was over.

On March 20, 1965, Dad received a letter from communist leaders that President Gheorghe had died the previous day. They asked Dad to present himself at his funeral, set for March 24, at Liberty Park, Bucharest, Romania (currently called Carol Park).

Only a few selected communists were invited to his funeral. Dad was a respected secretary communist among the thousands invited to the funeral. In fact, he was so respected that he appeared in the Drapelul Rosu newspaper, which meant, The Red Flag, and was shown throughout Romania. He was allowed to bring Mom as a plus-one to the funeral gathering.

On March 24, Dad worked early in the winter morning before dawn, dressed in his professional business attire and placed on his head a Panama hat. Both Dad and Mom left home to go to the funeral and left my sister, my brother, and me home alone again.

Mom and Dad were outside, ready to leave the property, but Mom stopped Dad from leaving because she had not prepared food for us. Dad, being in a hurry, demanded that they both leave because they were running late to catch the train. The ride was about an eight-hour commute to the location. Missing the train would cause a dent in Dad's busy schedule.

Once again, we starved, and the house lacked electricity and water. Mom did not prepare any food for us because Dad was rushing her to leave the house. We were put in a hazardous situation. The worst feeling was that we did not know when they would return home.

Who's to say they will grab dinner afterward or take a detour elsewhere while the three of us struggle to survive? I made myself responsible for my siblings and cared for them while my parents were away. The experience of being left home was very discouraging, and it left me feeling rejected because Dad did not bother to plan to take care of his own family. The three of us had a challenging time being left alone, not knowing where our next meal would come from.

However, before my parents arrived home, Grandma visited from Buziaş and took me back to her place again. I was twelve years of age at this time, so Grandma was happy to see me as a grown boy. Before Grandma decided to leave this house and return to Buziaş with me, she was concerned about why we were alone in the house without any food. She stayed with us for a few hours, then she and I left.

I always loved to be around my grandma, so I chose to leave but knew I would come to visit again for the summer.
Dad would not be happy when he found out I went to Buziaş with Grandma. I did not give him notice, given that I was the man of the house, until they got back.

When Grandma and I left for Buziaş, she also left some food for my sister and my brother that should last them for at least a few days.

During the afternoon, two days after Mom and Dad left, my sister heard the commotion coming from outside the house. She went outside to find Dad and Mom returning home from the funeral. My sister and brother came out to meet them, but they were both still far from the house.

My mom was disappointed to hear that my sister and my brother were alone at home. As they walked into the house,

Mom was more concerned about the kids' well-being. Dad walked past everyone without saying hello, as he continued to discuss with Mom who the next president of Romania would be.

Dad was concerned about the direction of this country instead of raising his own family. Mom rushed about the house, trying to feed and take care of the kids.

A few months later, I arrived back from Buziaș to visit during the summertime. I was extremely excited to spend time with Dad because I had not seen him for a while. I asked Dad if he wanted to play a game of soccer out on the street with me before the sun went down.

"Can't you see that I am busy, Viorel!" Dad yelled.

In my anger, I replied, "Just one game? The sun will go down soon!"

"Get out of here," he said. "I am discussing important affairs here!" Dad yelled with a look of threat on his face.

I cannot express the level of rejection I had at that moment. My chest began to feel heavy as I started to cry. Is it a crime to have a father figure in my life? All I wanted was to play soccer, I thought to myself. Hearing the commotion from Dad and Mom conversing in the kitchen, I decided to go to my room.

"How old are you? 12? And you are crying. I cannot believe this," Dad said with a scoff.

"Leave him alone," Mom insisted.

Mom stopped what she had been doing and walked me aside. I was having an emotional breakdown. She comforted me because I felt rejected by Dad.

"Let off some steam, Viorel," Mom suggested. "Dad just got home and has a busy schedule ahead of him."

"He is always like this, Mom. He never changes," I told her.

"Ever since he returned from the military, I've felt nothing but pain and rejection from him."

"He does not know you feel that way. Just do not talk back to him. You know not to do that," Mom demanded.

When Mom and Dad were in Bucharest, Dad purchased a brand-new television set. Mom did not tell me until now because she wanted Dad and me to build a better relationship.

"Tell you what," she said, "I have a surprise for you. Come follow me." So, I followed Mom into the family room where Dad was installing his new television set.

"What is that big black box, Mom?" I asked.

"Oh, just wait until Dad turns it on, and you'll find out," Mom said.

After several minutes, Dad finished installing the television, connecting the wires, and arranging the antenna. Dad turned on this anomalous black box, and suddenly, I saw my very first motion picture. I had never seen anything like this. Pictures were moving so fast. It was impossible to describe.

"This is a television, Viorel. We can now connect with the outside world and entertain ourselves," Mom said.

"Ask Dad if he wants to sit and learn about this television with you," Mom insisted.

"With him? Do you know what he just said to me a few minutes ago? No way!" I refused.

"Viorel, you wanted to spend some time with your father. This is your chance. Now go!" Mom demanded.

I had all the reasons in the world not to socialize with Dad, but I decided to talk to him anyway. I eventually asked him questions regarding this television, and to my surprise, he replied with an answer. I was blown away that Dad did not hurt me physically or verbally or have an outburst of anger towards me. I sat next to him and began asking more questions about the antenna above the television and how it works.

I knew nothing about televisions or antennas. Dad seemed willing to socialize when I talked about his interests. It made sense because he began installing this television when he arrived home from Bucharest, and I interrupted him. That's why he had an outburst of anger toward me.

When I asked him where he bought this television, he said he purchased it when visiting Bucharest. He mentioned that televisions, in general, are uncommon and hard to find. They can be awfully expensive, too. Then he explained how communists work here in this country.

Only people who were part of the communist party could purchase this television. Being part of the communist party, Dad became eligible to purchase it. In fact, one of the communist leaders who invited Dad to attend Gheorghe's funeral helped him buy it. People who refused to be part of the communist party were heavily restricted from acquiring various items, including television. Fortunately for me, my parents and my grandma played a role in the communist party, so I mostly had the necessities I need.

The only problem I had recently is that I continuously starve and thirst when my parents leave the house for an extended period of time without leaving enough food or water for us to live comfortably.

Socialism became heavy in this period, and the communist leaders wanted to run the country their way. Everyone and everything had to operate the same way. The only way to do that was to initiate socialism throughout the country. People who refused to become communists only prevented that from happening, so they were not permitted to enjoy having television, better-portioned foods, and more perks.

Therefore, the communists initiated the productivity-increasing policy, which meant that everyone, including communists, had to work more hours for the same pay rate. This allowed the people to get their minds off the corruption the communists were trying to develop and focus more on work.

On March 22, 1965, several guests, including some friends and neighbors, visited Dad. They came to watch television in the living room. Again, Dad was one of the very few people in the entire country who owned a television at this time, so we had plenty of people come to check this box out.

I remember watching television with everyone else when we saw Nicolae Ceausescu pronounced the new general secretary of the Romanian Communist Party. This made him the second Communist Leader of Romania.

Many of us hoped Nicolae would do better for us. Other people did not trust him because he was a former prisoner. Long ago, he was a member of the communist youth movement. Many in my community couldn't stop talking about his 1936 prison mugshot. It made them skeptical of him.

I was undoubtedly amazed at how I could view motion pictures from around the world and see them from my living room. Once Dad had this television, our family knew what went on across our country and the world. I never knew something like this was possible.

As more friends came into our home to watch television, a cousin of mine, whom I had never met, walked in with her parents. We were introduced for the first time; her name was Marcela. She lived in Buziaș.

My siblings and I wanted Marcela to become familiar with all the animals and scenery near our home.

"Here on this cow farm where we live, the beauty is endless," I said to Marcela.

I was willing to take Marcela on a quick tour of the farm to see many cows and the beautiful green fresh agriculture.

My sister, brother, and I spent time with her as we walked around the farm. The best part of this experience was picking mulberries from the trees. These berries have a naturally rich taste to them. It is something you can never imagine. These mulberries are sort of long, maybe about two inches long, and they look just as good as they taste.

Picking fruits from trees and walking around was something the four of us usually did on Sundays. We called it our Sunday Funday. Marcela would visit us on Sundays from time to time. She was very outspoken and extremely friendly. I enjoyed giving her this tour of different grass fields and flower fields.

As Marcela and I talked about agriculture, I found her to be a people person. She was very approachable with just about everyone she knew.

I felt compelled to stay at my dad's house because of the excitement of the television and the guests. However, I knew I would still much rather live with my grandma. At the same time, I also wanted to stay here to spend time with Marcela and travel around the village because she temporarily moved here to visit. It was a difficult dilemma, for sure. Marcela was from Buziaș, the same city where I grew up. It was nice to know that we both originated from the same city.

At some point, we decided to go outside and play tag or hide-and-seek games. When we decided to play hide-and-seek, we walked outside the village over to the grass field to play. Over there, you can see the green hills located miles away near the horizon just before sunset. It was breathtaking.

Marcela was the seeker, while my sister, brother, and I went away quickly to hide. Of course, my brother, being my brother, went climbing a huge full-grown Quercus Robur tree. My brother was concealed entirely due to the drastic number of leaves on that tree. Meanwhile, my sister and I wanted to be extreme, so we fled across the grass fields, about an eighth of a mile away, toward the cows.

"She will never find us here," I told my sister.

"Yeah, what is she going to do? Come here and ask the cows for clues about where we are," my sister laughed.

Ten minutes later and Marcela was not successful. Eventually, Marcela walked near the tree in which my brother was hiding. Moments later, a flock of red-breasted geese suddenly stopped inside my brother's hiding place for an important bird convention.

When my brother heard cluck noises, he became anxious as the sound approached him and became louder. Then, a multitude of cluck noises rippled across the field.
Marcela looked up at the tree, and she could hear many bird feathers flapping around as they settled on the branches.

Suddenly, my brother screamed, as many acorns, feathers, and leaves fell from the tree. My brother, covered in feathers, quickly worked his way down the tree.

"Okay! You found me!" my brother said to Marcela.

Marcela laughed and said, "No, I think those birds found you first."

Marcela asked my brother where my sister and I could be hiding, and then she heard a loud commotion coming from cows across the field. When Marcela and my brother listened closely and followed the cow sounds, they soon found many cows gathered on the field, and my sister and I flat on the grass, telling the cows to hush because they wouldn't stop mooing.

I looked up, and I saw Marcela looking at us.

"Wow, I didn't have to do anything to find you. The birds and cows can play better than we can," Marcela laughed.

"Cows have conventions, too? Who would have thought?" my brother joked.

"Well, we chose the worst time to play hide-and-seek," Marcela said.

It was dark outside. The sun had been down for a while now. We decided to head back home, and the four of us did what kids do, race home and laugh at the one who came in last place. There was a little dirt path that we found that led us home.

We were sort of scared because it was very dark behind us. There may have been some bushes beside us, and we didn't know what animal could pop out from there. Though my sister disagreed with racing, she caught us off guard and ran home without a count.

"Wait! We haven't started yet! Yelled Marcela called after her.

"I don't know what's behind those bushes! I'll see you guys if you make it back home," my sister teased.

My sister was quick-witted. She knew that the three of us were slow at running. If a scary animal jumped out of the bushes, my sister would try to have the slow runners behind her. We decided to race even though my sister got a head start.

Seeing the dirt path in front of us was challenging, but we had a full moon as our light guide. As we raced home, we would hear strange noises every now and again. Sometimes we laughed, and sometimes, we screamed in fear. It was a bittersweet experience because my brother was in last place, screaming in fear for us to stop running. But once we made it home, we had a great laugh and realized it wasn't so bad after all.

Of course, my sister had a head start. She stood in front of our home with her index finger over her chin.
She said, "What happened? I was waiting here all night. I had a late dinner, and you guys just now arrived?"

"Very funny. I'd like to see you in last place someday. You would be screaming, too." Marcela told her.

Our conversation amongst ourselves quickly ended as soon as we heard a commotion going on inside the home. Friends and neighbors who came to visit and watch television were just about ready to leave home. Marcela's family eventually left as well. It was great getting to see her for the first time.

[The FIFA World Cup story will contain an extensive series of detailed dialogue. If you feel no interest in this, please skip to chapter 5.]

A year later, on July 12, 1966, the FIFA World Cup was happening. My favorite team, West Germany, was competing against Switzerland. I was so excited to see this game. I loved soccer probably more than anyone in my family. Now that Dad had a television, I could view the game from home. It was a dream come true. It was almost impossible to see the FIFA World Cup four years ago because we did not have television and Romania had no connections to view the game from other countries.

Hungary, Yugoslavia, and other countries could connect to the World Cup soccer game, but in Romania, we were unable to. Dad and I placed an antenna over the house and directed it toward Hungary. That way, we could have a strong connection from outside the country.

Once we had everything set up, we could watch the game without a problem. I was in the room watching the soccer game with Dad and other friends and neighbors, who were communists. As I watched the game, I saw how West Germany quickly defeated Switzerland. I was cheering West Germany on, jumping, yelling at players loudly, telling them what to do as they ran across the field with the ball. It was almost as if I predicted their next move on the field, hoping that Haller would pull a scissors move on the defenders on the field and score a point.

Over an hour flew by, and West Germany had already scored four points, while Switzerland had zero points. Suddenly, our communist friends, Dad, and I, sat quietly and attentively as we saw what had just happened. West Germany was given the opportunity to kick a penalty goal. Time was running out; my eyes were locked on the television screen. These last penalty kicks would finish the game between West Germany and Switzerland.

"Come on, Haller! Make this kick!" I said anxiously. Player number eight, Helmut Haller, was standing twelve feet away from the goalpost. He took a few steps back from the soccer ball.

This is it. This is happening, I thought as I held my breath. I was biting my thumbnail with one hand and scratching the back of my head with the other. Haller goes for the kick. The ball goes flying and cuts through the air with unbelievable speed and trajectory.

The goalkeeper dives sideways with his arms stretched high. "GOOOAAALLL!" The commentary screamed as West Germany scored the penalty kick.

"BRAVO! We did it! I screamed out loud with joy." The entire house raged with cheer, and a roar of chatter and commotion as West Germany won the game.

"Noi am terminat!" Said one communist friend sitting to my right as he stood up with his jacket over his forearm. Many friends and neighbors quickly stood up from the couch and began chit-chatting for hours in the living room as they eventually prepared to leave the house.

Now that was a wild game. Though West Germany won five to none, it was still a good show. I never wanted Switzerland to score even one point. I was extremely impressed by West Germany. Helmut Haller was the most valuable player on the team. You should have seen how Haller poke-tackled Kurt Armbruster from behind as Kurt was shielding, and Max Lorenz instantly took possession of the ball. That was fun to see.

I realized this television was bringing Dad and me together. Before we had this television, Dad still loved and cared for me, but we did not have a strong bond until we started watching soccer together.

We were both cheering on West Germany and watching the soccer player's every move closely. Dad and I talked with each other without realizing it. I was delighted for us to finally have a common ground.

Once our communist friends and neighbors left the house in the late evening, Dad and I continued to recap what had happened in the soccer game. We discussed each player based on their performance during the game. Dad went on to tell me about the advantages and disadvantages of West Germany. We were forming brackets in our thoughts and predicting who would win the World Cup Finals based on West Germany players versus other countries.

While he was talking, I began to zone out for a second and think how happy I was to be in this conversation with my dad. Something like this does not happen all the time. I could agree and disagree with his thoughts about the game, and he was okay with it. I could not find the words to express how thankful I was for that moment. From the beginning, I wanted Dad to be a father figure and spend quality time with me. At this moment, I had that.

West Germany was scheduled to play Argentina on July 16. Dad and I were excited for that day because Germany continued moving forward in the 1966 FIFA World Cup.

When the day arrived again, many neighbors flooded into our home before the game started. I watched Argentine players walk out of the tunnel alongside West Germany players. The national anthem played, and the stadium attendees roared as the percussion band blasted their drums and symbols. The house echoed with commotion coming from the many guests visiting to see the game. It was a big moment for me because West Germany was moving forward.

The players on the field got into a formation, shoulder to shoulder, and the referee was just about to do a coin toss between two team captains. I could not sit still. I rubbed my palms back and forth, creating friction, just anticipating this moment.

The game began, and suddenly, the entire room went silent. I carefully examined and tried to predict every player's move. Thirty minutes went by and a constant fight over the ball kept the game scoreless. West Germany players had beautiful footwork, but Argentina came and took possession of the ball.

After a while, Dad and a couple of other people in the room began to shout out players' names and tell them what to do. We were over half way through the game and the score remained zero to zero. Time was running out; no one had a point, and I was losing my mind because West Germany took shots at the goalpost and missed multiple times. The ball was continuously kicked across the field, back and forth, and everyone in the room was frustrated.

Both teams did their best, and there were many excellent kick attempts. The game ended with no score. Seeing West Germany walk away with zero points was a serious disappointment. On the bright side, we knew West Germany would move forward to compete against Spain on July 20. West Germany had an excellent defense. That is one thing I took away from watching that game.

I was surprised to see West Germany move forward after playing so many games. Argentina had some really skilled players. I mean, both teams fought for that ball like mad dogs. The ball went flying recklessly over the field countless times. That game versus Argentina got my heart pumping like you wouldn't believe.

When July 20 rolled by, I found my place on that couch and was expectant of how West Germany would play this time. Communist friends come by to watch as well. The entire house was filled with loud chatter until the games finally started. Both teams came out of that tunnel and lined up on the field. After the coin toss, the game began, and everyone in the house watched closely as West Germany players fought for the ball. As the game continued for about twenty minutes, I was slightly discouraged to see how well Spain was doing. No one scored a point yet. However, Spain was very strategic and responsive and had beautiful footwork.

West Germany was able to take possession of the ball by poke tackling, but then Spain would intercept. So, it was just an ongoing battle over the ball, just like the game against Argentina. Suddenly Spain had possession of the ball again. They managed to run across the field and past the defense. I stood up as I watched. I could not believe what was happening. Willi! What are you doing? Get the ball! I screamed out loud. Willi Schulz played defense, and Spain flew right past him. Spain scored their first point. Spain players went running around and hugged each other as they celebrated. What a disappointment. I cannot describe how defeated I felt after seeing Spain score that point. I could have sworn that Willi would take possession of that ball, but to see him not take the ball was such a bummer.

Well, we could only hope for Germany to score the next point. As the game continued, I noticed how Germany passed the ball around more often than usual. German player Albert played as a midfielder and made such a great pass to another player. He guarded the ball very well, too. Then later they lost the ball.

Siegfried Held was on the sidelines, ready to throw the ball to one of his players near Spain's goal post. As Held threw the ball, Lothar Emmerich quickly came running and scored a powerful kick into the goalpost.

"GOOOAAALLL!" I screamed out loud, along with everyone else. What a great moment, we were now tied with Spain, 1 and 1. The pressure was on. My eyes were locked onto that screen to see who would score the next point.

The game progressed quickly, and I was nervous and sweaty because we were tied Spain. Anything could happen, and this would become anyone's game. As I looked at the television, something caught my attention. Siegfried Held had possession of the ball, and Spain player Manuel Sanchis quickly came to take the ball, but he fell. He got up quickly. Held dashed towards the goalpost as Sanchis sprinted alongside him and attempted to poke-tackle him from his right side. However, Held quickly passed the ball to Uwe Seeler, and he scored our second point, and that was the game!

On the television screen, the entire arena roared with cheering, and the players ran and scattered across the field with excitement. I began to jump up and down as Dad and his friends shouted and cheered.

We did it! I shouted. West Germany beat Spain, and they will move forward into the quarterfinals. I was so happy. My heart was beating so fast, and I felt energized to see West Germany win again! That was such a close game, it was very hard to watch, and now it is finally over!

On July 23, the quarterfinals began. West Germany and Uruguay played. I watched the entire game with Dad. Germany won the game, four to zero. That seemed like an easy win for us.

Haller played, and he made many passes and poke-tackled many of Uruguay's players in an attempt to steal the ball.

I was excited as West Germany continued with the World Cup Championships. All I could think about was seeing West Germany play at the finals and see them move forward in the game. It made my dad happy too.

On the morning of July 25, I started my day with a good breakfast. A loaf of bread is cut into slices with some Greek spread over it. I figured since Germany is playing Russia in the semi-finals this afternoon, I might as well start my day right. Dad and I continued to talk about Germany and Russia all that day. I told him that since Uwe Seeler was captain of the West Germany team, he would have Helmut Haller take possession of the ball most of the time. He was, in my opinion, the MVP of the team.

Dad disagreed and said everyone should take possession of the ball, not just Haller. If everyone takes possession of the ball, you are not limited to just one person. That is why there is a team, for everyone to work together.

I still disagreed with him on that point. Haller is an outstanding player, and for the past few games, Haller took possession of the ball most of the time, and they did very well that way.

"We'll see about that," Dad said.

Later that day, the semi-finals began, and West Germany played against the USSR. It was a good and fun game. West Germany won the game, two to one.

I was truly happy to see West Germany move to the finals. I ran around the house, did some push-ups, and then ran some more. Mom and Dad thought I was crazy for doing that, but I could not contain my excitement for West Germany.

The five days before the finals felt like five years for me. That's how badly I wanted to see the finals. England would play against West Germany, and I didn't think England would win the game. Germany had some talented players.

I asked Dad if we could go to London to watch the finals in Wembley stadium.

"Have you gone insane, boy? It's impossible to leave this country. We are under the Soviet communism regime," Dad yelled.

"But almost 100,000 people will attend. I want to be there, too!" I exclaimed.

"Go to your room! I'll spank you with my belt one hundred thousand times. How about that?" Dad replied.

Well, that did not work. It just doesn't seem fair how the government locked us inside this country. I don't even think we were allowed to use satellites to hear or see what's happening outside this country, including watching the FIFA World Cup.

It did not matter because we would watch it anyway. Nothing would stop me from watching the finals. If anyone knows me, they will understand that if I really want something, I go and get it, no matter what. Except for going to London, that would not happen.

As the finals approached, I looked at the England soccer players and viewed their previous performances in the World Cup. I noticed that Jacky Charlton and Bobby Charlton were brothers, playing on the same team. I found that interesting, considering it had been about twelve years since Germany had two brothers playing on their team in the World Cup in 1954. I chuckled after I realized that. Boy, this is going to be an interesting game.

The big day arrived, the day of the finals. Many friends, again, gathered at our home for the big day. I waited for the game to start, feeling butterflies in my stomach. Then, finally, it began! I turned up the television volume because of the loud voice chatter around me. The players came in through the tunnel, and soon the kick-off happened.

Watching this game was difficult because I did not want West Germany to make a mistake. After all, this was the final. I never wanted Peters, number sixteen, to take possession of the ball because his passes were very aggressive and accurate. Rarely was there ever an interception from his passes.

However, there was a tremendous development during the beginning of the game. West Germany took possession of the ball multiple times. Then suddenly, as I watched Sigfried Held pass the ball to an England player, he quickly lost possession. Haller rapidly stepped in when he saw a chance and kicked the ball. The ball came flying past many England players, including the goalkeeper. "GOOOAAALLL!" the commentary screamed.

Yes, West Germany scored the first point after fifteen minutes of the game. It was about time. I was disappointed to see West Germany not score a point after fifteen minutes. England scored their point after time so the score was even, temporarily.

According to Dad, England was not worried about being tied. Since the last three previous World Cups, the team that scored first lost. England thought that was the case for them. They hoped for their team to win.

England scored their second point as the game continued, which caught me off guard. How could this be? Especially after how well West Germany has been working as a team.

My hands began sweating when I realized this could be a challenging game. England was in the lead for a while. Fast forward to the end of the match, England had scored three points, while West Germany only scored two points.

I did not like where this game was headed because England was winning. The commentary said that it could all be over any second now. West Germany is fighting for the ball now, but

Hurst, the England player, took possession of the ball. He rand with the ball, with Wolfgang Overath tailing him from behind. All the attendees around the stadium stood up as they saw Hurst just twenty feet away with the ball. He made the shot and scored the final score.

"GOOOAAALLL!" Screamed the commentary while the stadium crowd roared after England's victory.

I was disappointed to see West Germany lose by only two scores. I could have sworn that the soccer ball hit the goalpost frame and only landed on the ground. I don't even think the ball hit the net. The game was stolen from us, and this did not make me a happy camper.

Overall, the entire World Cup was phenomenal, and I was extremely thankful that I was able to watch the game on the television, thanks to my dad. The most important part of this experience was to see a strong bond between Dad and me. We shared common ground, and I felt blessed to have had that time with him. I would have never thought that watching the World Cup with Dad could build the father-and-son relationship I desperately wanted. I even tried to play soccer with Dad, but he hardly ever wanted to spend time with me because he was too busy working on his other projects. He still cared, provided, and loved me from time to time, but I'd say that we grew closer while watching the soccer game.

5

BECOMING INDEPENDENT, 1973

My dad inspired me when I turned seventeen to find a career and make some good money. Dad taught me much about hard labor. I learned a thing or two from Dad:

- Be excellent at everything you do.
- Work hard.
- Never give up.

Those three are easier said than done, but I told myself I would pursue a promising career and excel at it. I was looking around, seeking which career path to take. One morning, I got up early to turn on the television and then made myself breakfast. Something on the TV caught my attention as I cut bread and vegetables.

There was communist propaganda on TV. The announcement was about lathe operators and their perks. A television reporter said that being a lathe operator is like having a golden brace on your wrist as a sign of achievement.

I listened intently because I was intrigued by what I heard. After hearing the reporter, I became interested in working as a lathe operator because I enjoy doing everything perfectly and excellently. Granted, working as a lathe operator is difficult. I would need to perform functions on large metal pieces that meet the appropriate criteria and specifications. It is physically demanding because you have to stand on your feet for several hours at a time. Nevertheless, I still desired to work as a lathe operator because I wanted to be challenged and look past the negative side of it.

I did some research on this position. I contacted the Professional School of Mechanics and enrolled in their program. It was called Uzina Mechanic Timișoara (UMT). This school was in downtown Timișoara, and they financed many school necessities for me so that I could graduate. The factory paid for the food, work clothes, schoolbooks, and classes.

The only catch was after I graduated, I had to work at the factory as a lathe operator for five years. I did not mind that at all. I was only concerned about learning the materials in class to pass and succeed. Staying mentally focused and remaining motivated was a considerable challenge for me because there were so many things to learn.

After about three years of study, I prepared for the final exams. I was nervous and felt unprepared even though I studied for hours, day in and day out. I had to learn how machines operate and problem-solve in challenging situations.

One night I went to the Timișoara Orthodox Metropolitan Cathedral, the most iconic building in all of Timișoara. I was alone in the Cathedral. I sat on the front row bench and began praying to God for help on this final exam. I thought maybe if I prayed, all the nervousness would go away.

A few hours later, I was still in the Cathedral. I still felt nervous about the exam, but I knew God was somehow listening. This exam was expected to be very difficult and intense. The Lathe Operating placement test had limited availability. Very few who took the test were admitted.

I did not know Jesus Christ personally at this time, but something stirred inside me while I talked to God, trying to receive help for this exam.

I left the building that night, but once a day for about a week straight, I returned to the Cathedral and asked God for mental support to pass the exam. Every time I prayed in that building, I felt different walking out those doors. It was the strangest experience because I felt like God had heard me.

When the final exam came about, I felt confident and ready to pass the test. I studied for weeks and did not get much sleep through it all. After I took the exam, I waited to see the results. Shortly, I received notice that I had passed the exam.

I will never forget how excited I was after I received the results. The exam was challenging. Not one section of the exam was easy. I graduated from UMT in May 1973 and began working as a lathe operator at the factory in Timișoara.

This has been a dream for me, and to live the dream blew my mind. I felt proud of myself because not many people graduated from this school, and I was just a twenty-year-old kid about to work as a lathe operator.

Days later, my name was listed on a chart in the school where I went to take the test. Very few people's names were listed there. I felt so proud of myself. This was an answered prayer from above because I would never have made it here alone.

Though schooling was arduous, the tasks in the workplace were straightforward. I was the best worker there and made very few mistakes. My performance at work was extremely precise. I was very quick. Everything I did had to be perfect.

I worked with a drill press and metal shear machines to cut thick steel metal. I used a lathe machine to quickly rotate a piece of metal, then cut and shape them according to their requirements. I prepared long metal shafts that were thirty feet long, designed to be used in large boats and ships.

Creating bolts and screws for ships and other transporting machines was an exciting experience for me. Ships contain many moving parts, and anything that can go wrong, will. However, having my fingerprints all over these parts is a huge privilege. I stayed motivated by having this one thing in mind: to take on an arduous task and execute it successfully and fast.

I desired to move to higher positions within the factory and take on new challenges. After working at the factory as a lathe operator for nearly three months, I realized I enjoyed every moment, especially since I was getting paid very well. The only negative side of this job was overworking. The government requires everyone to constantly work and never stop, which seemed suspicious. Something sketchy must be going on behind the scenes in this country.

In October 1973, after just three months at the factory, I was drafted into the military. I did not want to be drafted into the Army because my life was just beginning, but I had no other alternative. It happened so suddenly, without any warning or option.

When I presented myself to the recruiter and other military officials, they mentioned I would serve as a border patrol officer. I went through training and boot camp located in a small Bordertown, Comloșu Mic, just west of Timișoara.

We also prepared our station gear for our shift and reported to duty. I did not appreciate how the system was run in the military. The lieutenant and other high-level officials did not treat the trainees or me fairly. They would mock and criticize us and use condescending words towards us. Living through that sort of lifestyle was extremely uncomfortable. I was treated like a dog every day, and I felt invisible in the eyes of the lieutenant.

After completing boot camp and all the necessary military training, I officially began working as a border patrol officer. I had the graveyard shift because my lieutenant needed more eyes on the border. I was on duty with a few other officers patrolling the yard.

Operating as a border patroller was exceedingly terrible because it was freezing outside. The military disregarded me and did not care if I was freezing. I felt like my bones were ice, and there was no way to find shelter or a place of warmth. The lieutenant ordered me to be exposed and constantly present so no one could jump the border. The condition in Romania was deplorable. Many people tried to escape from the western part of Romania because communism was increasing, and many people desperately wanted to leave the country.

It was snowing in the middle of the night during many of my shifts, and falling asleep was not easy, especially when I was trying to keep warm. Captain Pietrarua, the night shift commander, occasionally peeked through our stations to ensure no one was sleeping. He commanded us to lay down on our bellies to be unseen for the entire shift regardless of weather conditions. By doing so, I could quickly spot anyone trying to escape over the border.

One night, I sat down against a building to keep warm and rest for a bit. I couldn't help but sleep because I was very cold and tired. I was exhausted to the point that my stomach began to ache, and I felt very nauseous. I worked twelve-hour shifts near the border from 7 a.m. to 7 p.m. It seemed like this service would never end.

I needed to sleep, but I knew it wasn't allowed. As I lay against the brick wall, I involuntarily fell asleep, suddenly jumping awake. I did that about five times for ten minutes. So, I started to do sit-ups for a few minutes to warm up my body and stay awake and warm. That did not help. I fell asleep again when suddenly, I heard the patrol dog barking loudly across the courtyard. I jumped awake again, and I felt my adrenaline rushing because I knew something was wrong. I went to see what had happened but found it hard to see as the light posts were shining a yellow, glaring light through the fog across the yard. I thought, who could jump the border during this foggy gloomy night?

It turned out the captain had come to check on us and see how we were doing. I was terrified, and I quickly stood up, put myself together, and yelled loudly, "HALT! Who are you?" I presented myself before the captain by crawling towards him. I reported to him that there had been no malicious activities during my mission.

"Is there something wrong, Mr. Matei?" asked the lieutenant.

I limped as I approached the captain because my right foot had fallen asleep. I did not know how to respond except to say, "No, Sir."

He continued inspecting everyone around the border to ensure no one was sleeping. The captain demanded that whenever he came to inspect us, we would yell out a secret passcode with a loud shout and tell him to stay back. We had a unique code that only we knew. He wanted us to respond in such a way so that we could be identified as patrolling officers and not suspects. We also had to keep thirty feet between us and the lieutenant or

Captain. Patrol officers had been killed by imposters disguised as patrol officers. That was why the captain instructed us to send out a code for the lieutenant.

Now, I was only getting eight hours of sleep per week. I was completely frustrated living under these conditions. Typically, when I finish my twelve-hour shift, I return to my dorm by train during the cold, snowy night. Before heading to bed, I was required to thoroughly inspect and clean my brand-new AK-47 rifle with cold water. Afterward, I washed the military dorm floors with my bare hands using a damp cloth. The dorm was about 550 square feet, so I quickly cleaned and dusted the walls before heading to bed.

As soon as I finished my chores, I laid my head to rest, and when I began to drift off to sleep, the alarm went off. A loud ringing noise permeated the entire dorm. Everyone jumped from their beds and rushed to put their uniforms on. Soldiers busted the front door open and began to scream, Everyone up!

We had three minutes to quickly shower, put on our uniforms and present ourselves to the commander. I felt completely disoriented and exhausted. I never got enough sleep. The Romanian military did not care that we did not get enough sleep, even though we had to work twelve-hour shifts. The military humiliated me, and I felt like a dog the entire time.

One night, when I went on to my night shift, I was drained, as usual. About five hours into my shift, the night shift captain appeared near us again. However, I was asleep on the floor on my belly. He walked around and found one of the border patrol officers sleeping. He kicked him a few times and told him to stand up. I woke up, witnessing the scene.

Shortly after that, I fell asleep again. The captain approached me and said with a loud, croaky voice, "Matei, where is your code?" I suddenly woke up as he said those words.

I told him I wanted to be silent so I would not become a target. He did not know that I was asleep. Although what I told him was not entirely true, he regarded my statement and claimed my reaction to be profound. I was shocked that Captain Pietrarua did not kick me because he was known for kicking patrol officers who fell asleep.

The next day, the night crew captain and the day crew lieutenant called for an important meeting in the boardroom. We presented ourselves at the meeting, and the captain came to make some necessary changes to our code and protocols. He mentioned that we would no longer have to yell out a secret password when a trespasser appeared. Instead, we will need to remain silent to avoid becoming a target.

He said, "Last night, when I went to check the fields to see if all the soldiers were down on their bellies and not asleep, I stopped at Viorel. He did not shout. He just used his soft voice. From now on, we will no longer shout. We should confirm quietly, instead."

I was surprised to hear the captain say those words. Because of me, a new rule had been established in the military border patrol.

I continued to secure the border, and I began to build traps hidden under the dirt. These sound traps prevented intruders from fleeing or trespassing into Romania. When the intruder stepped on the springs, they would try to untangle themselves. The springs, connected to a loud bell, would then signal with a loud sound, and lights would also flash across the yard so that we would know an intruder was present.

After seven months in the military, in May 1974, I developed pleurisy. I had severe inflammation surrounding my lungs, which gave me terrible pain, especially when doing physical activities. It started happening during my annual training. The drill chief commander overworked us to the point where we all almost had hypothermia.

He gave out orders during physical training. We were out in a large field full of snow. It was early in the morning, my bones were freezing, and my fingertips were completely numb. My mind was not thinking straight. My blood was becoming thick, and it was difficult for me to use my hands for physical activities. All the soldiers were in formation, ready to receive orders and perform for this training.

The chief would yell his orders loudly, and we must comply. He would tell us when to drop, when to get up and when to run. His orders were repetitive and demanding. He spoke condescending words over us and made us feel extremely humiliated.

He did not care about our physical health. We never stopped, even if we were thirsty, hungry, or tired. The chief was selfish; the entire management was corrupt. Then we were ordered to run from one village to another in extremely cold weather, and we never stopped.

During one run, when we made it to the other village, I was so thirsty from the physical training that I ran to a cold fountain and drank a large amount of iced water. My fellow trainee said, "Stop! Don't drink too much cold water while your body is heated. You can get sick."

I didn't listen; I kept drinking, eventually becoming sick. When I inhaled, I could hear and feel water bubbles down my lungs. I was in such pain I cried and begged for a nurse. I reached out to my commander for help. I even tried to go to the nurse, but the commander didn't care. He wanted me to keep training. This commander was selfish.

The next day, I was taken to a doctor in Jimbolia, a city in Romania located in a border town. The doctor did an x-ray and diagnosed me with pleurisy. After his diagnosis, they sent me to a military hospital, holding me for treatment for 45 days. They gave me special treatment to protect my lungs and help me breathe properly.

Shortly after that, I was taken in for surgery. They made a small incision on my lower back and drew water out of my lungs. In 1974, the commander decided to send me home for four years as a discharge to recover. They said they would check on my health in about four years and determine if I should finish my service. I was due to complete ten more months in the military since I was discharged.

After arriving home to my parents in Bacova, I watched television with Dad on March 28, 1974, and saw that Nicolae Ceausescu was to become the first President of Romania.

The news spread across the country. Some people liked him, but others did not because he was building a good relationship with America's president, Richard Nixon. As soon as he was in office as president, he began to build many warehouses and other manufacturing facilities across the country.

Little did anyone know that he was borrowing funds from foreign countries. President Ceausescu was on a path toward years of financial misplanning and incompetent industrial development that would eventually hurt Romania's economy. He had a plan, and if he followed through with this plan, it would eventually make this country the second poorest country in Europe.

Dad was very concerned about what he heard on television. He disagreed with what President Ceausescu was planning. Romania was doing somewhat okay, but Ceausescu would make it worse by bringing Romania into deep national debt.

I stayed with my parents until February 1978, then moved to Buziaș to live with my grandmother again.

One morning in Buziaș, I went for a walk at the nearby park and met a girl. She seemed very friendly and approachable.

We began talking, and both felt a strong bond developing between us. She will remain anonymous for the sake of this book.

Days went by, and we continued to meet up at the park. After a while, she would come over to Grandma's house. Grandma noticed our connection. She knew we had become very good friends. Sometimes she would be at Grandma's house and wait for me to arrive home from work. Other times she would wait for me at the park so we could walk around and spend time together. She was very interested in me and had a servant's heart.

Grandma soon had a chance to meet her mother at the park. I was too shy to make the next move, so Grandma took the initiative and spoke with her mother about her and me. Grandma told her mother that we had developed a strong friendship and that we should start dating. Her mother was okay with that because she loved how I presented myself to her and the girl. I was always kind, honest, and caring.

One day I came home from work, and Grandma came up to me and said I might have a chance to date this girl and marry her soon.

We began dating for a while, and later, we married. We received our marriage certificates, and we were all set. The only thing is, we did not move in together.

In October 1978, I was called back into the military. My health returned to normal, so I went to finish the last ten months of my service.

A couple of months into my service, I noticed that my wife did not respond to my phone calls or letters. I became distraught that maybe something had happened to her. Weeks and months went by, and still no reply.

Grandma contacted me and told me she had been going out with other men and doing her own thing. She did not care about me anymore, and I never saw her again. It was almost as though we had never met.

I could not express the level of rejection I had felt at that time in my life. There was nothing much I could have done because I was away, serving in the military. I felt very sorry for putting myself in this relationship. I was willing to start a committed relationship with her, but she was not honest with me. My deepest desire was to have a wife who cared for and respected me.

Going through this difficult experience was a negative turnaround for me. I knew deep inside that everything would be okay, even though my mind was telling me otherwise. Honestly, I felt terrible the entire time I was in service.

Once I finally finished my time in the military in July 1979, I was able to figure my life out. I did not see my wife anywhere. I hadn't spoken to her when I arrived back home.

I continued working for the Uzina Mechanic of Timişoara (UMT). The manager suggested I apply for an apartment residence since I worked there. I thought that was a huge step for me to take in life. I was 29 years old when I moved into my apartment.

The reason why my manager encouraged me to apply for an apartment was because I was married. I had my marriage certificate, but I never reported my divorce from my wife. No one knew. So, I was eligible to apply for an apartment. Only married employees of UMT were allowed to apply. According to the communist regime, married employees needed to have a place to live and be comfortable. Doing so will enable them to keep working and not leave. I was quite surprised by this perk because usually, only communists were given such privileges. However, surprisingly, employees there, who were married, did not need to be a communist to have an apartment. This was the only bright side of the communist regime in Romania.

So, I went to apply for an apartment in Timișoara because my work was nearby. Soon I would not have to commute from Buziaș by train. In 1982, I was approved to be a resident in my new apartment. I moved into a 200-square-foot studio apartment. It was quite small, but it was just what I needed.

I had a good income working at the UMT factory as a lathe operator. My monthly income was around four thousand Lei, which converts to $925 US per month. That may not seem like a ton of money at this present time, but during the 1980s, it was considered high income.

After moving from Grandma's house and into my new apartment, I hired a painter to paint the walls in my room. I purchased new furniture and everything else I needed to live comfortably. I literally had everything. All I needed was a wife with whom I could share my life. I wanted to make sure that I had my life in order. By doing so, I could start a new family someday and eventually flee this country and have freedom.

6

FINDING CHRIST, 1984

I continued to work at the UMT factory. I started to feel lonely because I was the only person living in the apartment. The only friends I had were my co-workers. I was an introvert and did not branch out to meet new people.

One day I was relaxing in my room, watching television, when I realized one of my co-workers, Glitea, attended church regularly. I thought about asking him if I could attend church with him so that I could meet new people. So, the next day, I asked Glitea if I could go to church with him on Friday. He thought that was a great idea. He said he would pick me up.

I felt a sense of relief after asking to go to church with him because I was timid to talk to other people. My only intention was to meet new people and make new friends at church. I did not intend anything more than that. Growing up, I had some knowledge about God but did not have a spiritual lifestyle. I was not planning on living a spiritual lifestyle. I did not even think about that. I was only hoping that once I made new friends, I could have people over to my apartment to eat food and hang out.

When Friday night arrived, I dressed up and stood outside waiting. An hour passed, and Glitea had not arrived to pick me up. After standing outside for such a long time, I felt rejected. I did not feel included with everyone else at church.

"Maybe Glitea changed his mind about me," I thought. My mind was racing with all sorts of made-up scenarios that only encouraged me to feel even more rejected.

So, the next day, a Saturday, I went to work. I spoke with Glitea and asked why he did not pick me up yesterday. Glitea told me that he forgot to pick me up, and instead, he went out to play a gig with his band. I expressed my frustration with him and told him how incompetent he was for having me wait outside alone for two hours.

I also asked him a rhetorical question. I said, "What kind of Christian are you?"

While I was talking to Glitea, another one of my co-workers was eavesdropping on our conversation. His name was Ghita Alecsei. He worked on a huge piece of metal, but he stopped what he was doing and came up to Glitea and said, "You need to apologize to this man and help him out. You need to own up to your mistakes."

Glitea admitted his wrongdoing. He apologized to me. He realized what he had done could have kept me from knowing Jesus Christ.

If I had never spoken to Glitea about what he had done, I would have never known he had just forgotten to pick me up. If that were the case, I would never have gone to church again. I would have thought every Christian was similar, which is not true. I understood that he had made a mistake, and I appreciated his honesty and apology.

However, for some reason, my faith still stood firm. I knew that there was something new for me in my future, so I did not give up. I wanted to attend church to see what this was all about. Then Ghita Alecsei offered to pick me up and take me to a youth Bible Study on Tuesday night. He said he would be sure to wait for me this time, unlike the other incompetent guy over there. (Ghita said that loud enough for Glitea to hear him.)

I believed Ghita Alecsei because he was very polite, caring, and confident. So, 1983 was the year I started attending church regularly.

When Friday evening arrived, I quickly put on some nice clothes and waited outside my apartment for Ghita. I was unsure how to present myself in front of other people at the Bible study.

I thought I would not stand out too much if I wore nice clothes. I felt some pressure. I was nervous about being recognized and introduced by people I did not know. As I stood and waited in front of my apartment, I created many scenarios of how the Bible study would turn out. I hoped that Ghita would stay next to me the entire time because I was nervous.

When Ghita arrived, we headed to Bible study. I was thankful that he did not forget about me. As we were on our way, I allowed him to get to know me more, and I also began to learn more about him.

Ghita seemed like a very nice person. He seemed very intelligent. He mentioned he was studying to become a pastor. His goal was to earn multiple degrees in college and equip himself with knowledge so he could do what God had called him to do. Ghita was very considerate and selfless. I felt very thankful to know Ghita because he was very driven.

When we arrived at First Baptist Church or Biserica Nr. 1, I noticed many high school and college students. They were very energetic and polite. Many came in groups and had backpacks on while holding a notebook in their arms.

Everyone there kept talking about Jesus Christ. They seemed so passionate for Him.

Ghita was always next to me. He supported me and introduced me to many students at the church. Everyone there knew I was new at the church. They came to me with a smile and introduced themselves to me. This was totally different from what I expected. I thought no one would recognize me, but that was just in my mind.

When the Bible study began, we learned and discussed the book of Genesis. The speaker spoke very well concerning this book. I was very interested in this study because they talked about some profound insights concerning the creation of the world and the different characters within the book. To my surprise, I enjoyed every moment of the Bible study because the group leader spoke very well. He seemed funny and approachable, so listening to him speak about God's Word was entertaining.

The speaker did not use fancy big words or complicated illustrations. The speaker kept everything simple for everyone to understand.

The service was over, but I wanted to come back next week because I enjoyed the youth Bible study service. I was drawn to return because I was very interested in the Bible teachings. I looked forward to next week's service because everyone recognized me and was very polite. These people were much nicer to me than my other friends, who did not know Jesus Christ.

The friends I knew at work used profanity in their speech. They were not very nice to me. I continued to go to First Baptist Church regularly for about two years. I felt like this church was my home. I felt like I belonged here. In 1984, I attended First

Baptist Church for a revival service. Pastor Paul Negrut was a guest speaker from another church. God used his words to draw me near to Jesus Christ. His words impacted me as I was sitting in service.

Pastor Paul was very good at making the Word of God relevant to today's current events and other statistics on abortion and marriage facts. Hearing him speak made me look at what was happening in this country and understand the Bible is relevant to all that is happening regardless of how old the Bible may be.

As he began to wrap up the service, he ended with an altar call. He welcomed anyone to come up front who was willing to surrender their life to Jesus. I felt compelled to surrender my life to Jesus Christ that day. This was a big decision because I knew I would never be the same after Jesus.

I was nervous to walk to the front. My hands were sweaty and shaking. Eventually, I built up enough courage to get up and walk to the front. I knew I only had one life to live, and only Jesus could help me make the most of it.

Looking back, I realized that a few more people came up to the front with me, so I knew I was not the only one at the altar, which made me feel less nervous.

Pastor Paul turned to me and prayed over me. He seemed very polite and approachable and guided me through a prayer that would allow Jesus to be Lord over my entire life. He mentioned a passage in scripture from Romans 10:10. For it is by believing in your heart that you are made right with God, and by confessing with your mouth, Jesus is Lord, that you are saved.

I believed that with all my heart as I prayed. I had never felt such peace before as I did that day. I felt like I had removed a heavy leather jacket and placed on a new white jacket. The Bible talks about replacing the spirit of heaviness with a garment of praise. I believe that is what happened as I surrendered my life to

Jesus. I felt like a new person, as though a shining liquid light washed over me and made me clean.

After surrendering my life to Jesus Christ, I could not understand his grace and mercy. There are many terrible things I have done in my life. One of them was a few years back when I was at a very low place in life, and I was very upset with God because of my living conditions in this country. I was not able to stand living under communism any longer.

I walked outside during the night, looked up at the dark, purple night sky filled with many beautiful stars, and looked at God with an outburst of profanity. So, as I look back to that time, I thank God that he did not strike me dead. Jesus had a plan for my life and forgave me for what I did because I did not know what I was doing. I am so thankful to Jesus for doing what he did in my life. He deserves all the glory, not me, because I should have been long gone.

After the church service was over, I walked up to Pastor Paul. I spoke with him for a while to better understand his life story. I was completely intrigued. Pastor Paul had my eyes and ear's attention as he shared his experience in school. He mentioned that after graduating high school, he was curious to attend the University of Bucuresti.

Paul wanted to attend that university, so he began to fast food and water for days to receive help from God. He knew God would hear Him if he sought the Lord with all his heart. Paul was brilliant, so he did not study much for his placement test. He just walked in and began to write during his placement writing portion. He also took other subjects.

He mentioned that the Holy Spirit led him as he worked on his tests, with perfect scores on all of them. Paul was very influential among his peers because he accomplished many things at a young age.

Finding Christ, 1984

I was amazed to hear that God helped him through school in such a way. I mean, this was the God that I now served. I also felt very fortunate to have met Pastor Paul. It was such an honor to speak with him and have him pray over me.

As I walked out to the parking lot of First Baptist Church, many young adults came up to me and began talking with me. They were excited that I gave my life to Jesus, and they wanted to get to know me and spend time with me in fellowship. I felt accepted at this church because no one left me alone. There was no drama or gossip in this community. I made this place my home church.

Some mentioned that they would begin to pray and fast that I would get baptized soon. I am not a very social person, but I tried my best to spend time with these amazing friends outside of the church. I was very thankful to have known them and to have them in my life, mainly since I lived alone in an apartment. I desperately needed friends.

I had a strong desire to be baptized in water at my church. I did not know anything about baptism or its purpose. So, one night, I consulted my friend Ghita Alecsei, and I had him explain to me about baptism before I went further on this journey.

He told me baptism should be done before witnesses at your church because you are sharing with others the outward expression of your inward change, expressing what happened in my heart after I surrendered my life to Jesus. When someone is baptized, their pastor submerges them in water. Doing so serves as a symbolic image of your past sins being forever buried and washed away by the blood of Jesus.

There is more going on in the spiritual realm aside from this expression. God begins to create a new beginning in my life, a fresh start.

After hearing this from Ghita, I felt strongly compelled to get baptized immediately. I wanted to get baptized because I knew that I had not been living for God, but I had been living for myself. I knew I would need to be committed to living righteously for Jesus after baptism. Now that I have changed into a new person, I want to encourage others through my new decision by following Jesus.

The only thing is, I did not want my father to know that I was deciding to get baptized. If he found out, he would be agitated because his reputation as a communist would be jeopardized. Communists do not like people becoming Christians because it means they are making an intelligent decision in life. Communists want everyone to think the same, so no one will try to gain power and overthrow the communist regime. So, if I were to get baptized, I preferred to have it privately.

When the time came for me to get baptized at church, it was May 6, 1985. I had plenty of support from my church friends. They knew I needed a private baptism so no one would say a word to my father about this event. I was excited to get baptized because this was a new beginning. I anticipated what my future would look like now that Jesus Christ was in charge. The pastor took me up front, spoke some words over me, and baptized me in water.

After rising from the water, I had never felt so free in my entire life. I was not just taking a bath. I felt new inside my heart. If I were baptized without believing in Jesus, I would be taking a free bath. From this day forward, I took my faith seriously. I also began to study the Word of God more often.

My mom was the only person outside my church who knew I had received baptism. She kept it a secret for a very long time. When she heard this news, she was astonished. Mom understood the difficult challenges I had gone through in my childhood; she was amazed to see me grow and find my way to Jesus Christ.

She also visited my apartment for a couple of nights once and noticed how serious I was about reading and studying the Holy Bible. So much so that she decided to dedicate her life to Jesus Christ. She had some knowledge of various scriptures and God, as you may know from my childhood experience with scripture.

Mom never had a personal encounter with Christ until she saw how serious I was for Christ. She loved how determined I was to be baptized and to pursue the Lord Jesus, and she felt compelled to surrender her life to Jesus.

Mom also understood the risk involved with this decision because her husband, Stefan, might find out about this news. Mom did not let this concern her because this was something she really wanted. After this, Mom and I began to get involved in church and developed a deeper relationship as mother and son.

A couple of years passed, and I continued to attend church and grow in fellowship with my friends from church. I also grew closer to Jesus and learned new insights about God's truth in his Word.

One insight comes from the Gospel of John in the Bible. John 3:16 For God loved the world so much that he gave his one and only Son so that everyone who believes in him will not perish but have eternal life. This passage really resonated with me because I experienced the power of God when he came into my heart. I do not deserve salvation, yet Jesus gave up everything for me. This will forever be my favorite verse in the Bible, as common as it is.

One day, news came that Billy Graham would visit Romania to speak at the Timișoara Orthodox Metropolitan Cathedral.

The word spread across the entire country that he would speak. Finding a reservation for a seat to listen to him speak was a big deal. It seemed nearly impossible to find a way to make it to his service because it would be completely booked.

I do not understand how Billy Graham and his team managed to come and speak here in Romania. The communist regime in this country was very strict and did not allow religious figures to provide an event such as this. They were against strong religious practices and did not want people outside this country to come and influence the Romanian people. Although Romania had a longstanding history of religious influence, atheism had been strongly promoted by the communist government since World War II, and it had taken over Romania.

Religious commitment was discouraged because of what the communist government had done to this country. Billy Graham, however, was empowered by God and felt compelled to fulfill the great commission. He did not let this stop him. Because of God's favor, he was given a way to preach salvation through faith in Jesus Christ openly.

Billy Graham received an invitation from all churches throughout the country, which at the time was the most remarkable thing Billy had ever experienced in any country in the world.

On the day Billy Graham prepared to arrive and share the gospel message, the street in front of the Metropolitan Cathedral was filled with people five hours before his arrival. The entire building was filled to its fullest capacity. Crew members were outside setting up the speakers in front of the building so that the large overflow crowd on the streets could also hear Billy's message. There was an overflow of over one hundred thousand people camping outside the building.

Finding Christ, 1984

Many people began fighting, pushing, and shoving to make their way into the building. Though it was impossible to make their way into the Cathedral, many still tried to fight their way inside.

One hour before Billy Graham arrived, I showed up and waited outside. I observed what seemed like a man trapped, sandwiched between two large men. Many kept pushing each other, and this man could not make his way through the packed crowd. He cried for help because he was unable to move or breathe comfortably. I tried to go and help him, but I was also stuck in the crowd, unable to get by. That man began to scream louder and louder for help. It seemed like no one cared for that man. Unfortunately, I had no way to get to him. I could see and hear him, but the crowd was tight and ruthless.

Billy Graham arrived, escorted by his team into the building. The crowd started roaring and celebrating him as he made his way through those doors. I was desperate to make my way into the building, but it seemed impossible. The church was already full, and I felt discouraged even cutting through the crowd outside. The front door was still far off, but suddenly I felt motivated to get into the building. I fought my way through the crowd, working my way through the mass of people. It was the most difficult thing to do. I did not know how all these people could be so energetic about Billy Graham.

After twenty minutes of fighting through the large crowd on the streets, I finally managed to get into the front door. I made it inside the building. I sat around the corner of the room and saw Billy Graham standing behind the podium, preparing his message. I was eager to hear him speak.

Once his message began, everyone kept silent. It was the most remarkable experience I have ever witnessed. Not one voice spoke in the congregation, not one baby cried, and no distraction or ambiance erupted across the room. Everyone listened intently as Billy made his introduction behind that podium.

I was amazed at Billy because of the way he made his introduction. He did not introduce himself; he introduced Jesus Christ and his gospel to the people. He made known the purpose of his visit that night. It was that someone would come to know Jesus as their Lord and Savior. He did not speak as one with intellectual capability or to gain the interest of the people. His words seemed tangible. I felt the love of Jesus in every word he spoke. It was as though I was alone in a living room, chatting one-on-one with him. His words were simple, not complicated, or hard to understand.

Billy Graham began his sermon by telling a story from 2 Kings chapter 5 about a rich and great commander and king of Aram named Naaman. Although he was mighty and wealthy, he was severely ill with leprosy. His physical condition grew worse and worse by the day. A young girl working as a maid in his home told Naaman about a prophet in Israel that could heal him. His name was Elisha.

So Naaman left and went to Israel. When he arrived, he received a letter from Elisha instructing him to dip himself seven times in the Jordan River, and then God would completely heal him.

When Naaman read that letter, he hopped onto his horse and rode away in a rage. He claimed that Abana and Pharpar, the rivers of Damascus, were much cleaner than the rivers of Israel. Naamans servant caught him just in time and said, Naaman, if the prophet had told you to do something great, would you not have done it? How much more when he tells you to do something simple, to wash in this river seven times? Then, Naaman turned back and went to the Jordan River.

His friends laughed behind his back as Naaman prepared to dip himself in the water of Jordan. He dipped himself in the water once, then twice. He felt ashamed and saw no meaning in this. He then dipped himself up to seven times. Finally, when he dipped himself the seventh time, he got up from the water and was completely healed.

Billy Graham used this simple story to illustrate how we can do the same. Jesus asks us to do something simple. Many people overthink salvation and turn to work, hoping to earn salvation. But, with simple faith as small as a mustard seed, you can be healed, saved, and find freedom, only in Jesus Christ. It doesn't take much to follow Christ. It's a simple thing.

Many attend church faithfully. Many have a cycle of prayer throughout their day. Billy mentioned that everyone there that night could experience Jesus in a new way, in a very simple, powerful way, and have a personal companion with them all day long. He continued with his sermon, and I was amazed by the presence of God in the room. I had never experienced the power of God as I did that day. Many people were blessed by his message, and God used Billy in a powerful way to speak to the Romanian community in Timișoara.

As Billy Graham continued his sermon, I heard the commotion and a loud cutting noise coming from outside. I couldn't help but go out to see what was happening. I found the communist secret police cutting the speaker wires outside the building. They did this so that the overflow of thousands of people standing outside the building could not listen to Billy's message. The crowds were upset by that fact. One of Billy Graham's staff members heard this negative incident and reported this to Radio-Free Europe because, at that time, his staff had cell phones to make calls.

Once the message finished, Billy Graham left and received a tour of the rest of Romania. Some communist leaders took him sightseeing.

I saw Billy Graham close, in person, once. I was about twenty-five feet away from him as he walked down the hallway. He was taller than I had imagined and seemed to be a very confident man of God.

FLEEING FROM ROMANIA, 1987

After Billy Graham and his team made their departure from Romania and headed back to the United States, I became very depressed. I hated to see the Americans leave this country. During Billy's visit, he and his team brought positive energy and joy amid a sickening, ruthless, as dead as a doornail regime.

I started to think about freedom. It was all I could think about for days. I dreamt of living a perfect life in America, where I could lead my family in peace and freedom.

I felt compelled to find an escape from the Soviet satellite country. Making that a reality seemed very easy because I became sick and tired of living under the soviet communism regime.

There has to be more to life than this, I thought.

In August 1987, I decided to flee the country of Romania once and for all. I was going to leave, and no one was going to stop me. I knew fleeing the country would involve significant risks, including jail or even losing my own life.

I was willing to take that risk. I was courageous for my freedom. I was ready to fight, even if it killed me. I called for three of my closest friends to come along: Giuca Voicu, Chiruta Joan Alias (Ringo was his nickname), and Tudose Liviu.

The four of us left the city of Timișoara by car and arrived at a border village in the western part of Romania. We planned to start our journey when the sun went down so the village residents would not know we were there. If a villager spotted us, they would complain and call the border patrol soldiers to come and take us away.

The border-town villagers were ruthless and eager to turn anyone in who tried to cross the border. The communists did not allow outsiders in this village town because they did not want anyone to flee the country by passing through this village.

We made our way through the village at night and arrived at the border successfully. We began to plan our escape by using a large paper map. We planned to pass the western border of Romania safely and then arrive in Serbia. Once we arrive in Serbia, we can find our way to Italy, which is the best way to fly to America.

Many people went to Italy because planes were taking off from there to land in America. We established our plan and were more than ready to start our escape. We made our way closer to the border, but as we approached the border, we had to pass through a large 100-acre cornfield. The four of us quietly stooped down as we tried to make our way through the cornfield. It was not an easy task because many border patrol soldiers were scattered across the entire cornfield, lying down and one hundred meters apart.

The four of us were extremely nervous as we quietly separated the 6-7 feet tall corn stalks and made our way through the cornfield. There were many tall corn stalks and no paths. We could not see what a couple of feet was ahead of us, let alone being in the dark. A soldier could be lying in front of our path, so we were constantly alert and terrified for our lives.

Hours went by. I was surprised that we were able to last through the night. The sun began to rise. It was early in the morning, and we were still stooping down and quietly walking through the field.

During our trip, I carried ham, bread, and a generous portion of garlic cloves in a bag I brought from home. I also took with me a Holy Bible, which I kept. It was very precious to me. I did not plan to stay in this cornfield for longer than a few hours, so there was no need for extra food to carry around, but the garlic cloves Mmm, they were delicious, so I kept a couple of cloves in my pocket for later, then threw away the rest.

Hours had passed; my back and legs hurt from walking and stooping down for so long. My friends and I became extremely hungry and thirsty as we had not drunk water nor eaten before this escape. This mission became a drag because we were severely exhausted due to a lack of sleep.

At about 8 p.m., we heard a strange noise coming from the distance. The four of us stopped and listened carefully. We hoped it wasn't one of the patrol soldiers coming to chase us down. They could throw us in jail or even shoot us if we were caught. They had permission to shoot us dead on the spot.

Several minutes passed, and we hadn't heard that strange noise, so maybe we were mistaken about what we heard. A few minutes later and it was still perfectly quiet as we carefully took one step at a time through the cornfield.

I turned and asked Ringo, "Hey, what do you think that sound was a while ago?"

He replied humorously, "If it wasn't the sound of a Coca-Cola bottle opening, then we are in trouble."

Ringo was right. He had no soda bottle in his little pocket inventory. I suspected that sound to be from one of the patrol soldiers. I worried because maybe they were watching us, and we didn't know.

It was beginning to get dark again. I didn't think they had seen or heard us. I thought we might be okay.

Suddenly, we heard a car engine roar, blazing through the cornfield aggressively at high speeds. What did we do wrong? We were tremendously stealthy! How could this occur? The noise became louder and louder as the large military Jeep approached us recklessly at incredible speed, with its bright high-beam headlights reflecting off the corn stalks.

My buddies and I became terrified as we felt adrenaline rush through our bodies. We booked it as fast as we could. We were terrified at that moment. I began to get chills across my forearms and back from the fear and terror I was experiencing. My heart was pounding so hard. I became distressed and afraid, not knowing what would happen next.

We began sprinting through the corn stalks as fast as we could. We were shaking uncontrollably. We tripped, fell, and tramped over each other constantly as we got back up and continued through the cornfield, continually looking back in terror. It turned out that there was a watchtower a couple of miles away.

A soldier probably announced movement in the cornfield. The soldiers were like owls; they saw every little movement, even at night.

The military Jeep drove through the cornfield in a zig-zag pattern, trying to locate us, as the vehicle flattened and destroyed over 30 acres. My mind was going crazy. I was trying not to get myself killed by these communist demons. The driver was very reckless. He did not care if he mistakenly ran us over and killed us on the pitch-black night. They were allowed to do whatever they wanted. This shows how terrible, careless, and incompetent the communist regime was.

The four of us continued to run without a sense of direction. We just needed to get away from that monstrous Jeep. We were lost, not knowing where we were going.

Suddenly, to my right, I spotted something in the dark, like a large trench or a canal that stretched across the cornfield.

"Guys," I whispered louder than I wanted, "There's a canal."

We dove into the canal, thinking it was filled with water, but it was completely empty. Disoriented after the fall, I quickly used my hands to locate the canal walls. The canal was about ten or fifteen feet deep, with a 35% slope on either side. The four of us pressed our backs against the canal wall to hide from the driver's view as they might pass by.

We heard the Jeep in the distance, trampling over corn stalks and causing major damage to the cornfield. My friends and I were safe in the canal for now. We tried to catch our breath.

I asked my friends, "How did we not trample over a single patrol soldier while running across the field?"

As I mentioned, many border patrol soldiers lay on their bellies and scattered across the cornfield, one hundred meters from each other.

Giuca Voicu responded in anger, I don't know, but we need to get out of here. We're not going to make it out alive. It was quiet for a while. The Jeep military vehicle seemed to have de-escalated. We found ourselves in a state of regret and confusion.

My biggest regret was that I thoughtlessly threw away the ham, bread, and the precious garlic cloves I carried along.

Our plan seemed to have failed, and we found ourselves in the center of the cornfield (AKA) lion's den, longer than we intended. Hungry, I began to ponder about the food I once had. Why did I throw that food away? What was I thinking?

We were clueless about how we would get out and escape safely. Short of breath, Ringo said, "This is a bad idea. Why are we doing this?"

"Look around you, Ringo," I said. Look at what's happening to us right now. It's all because of these evil communist rats that this is happening. Do you want to live like this for the rest of your life, Ringo?" I asked.

Ringo was disappointed in the situation because it was more difficult than he expected. But I was never going to give up. I was willing to fight and make it to Serbia, regardless of how scared, hungry, tired, or hopeless I felt.

After ten minutes of us laying with our backs pressed against the canal wall, no one said a word, and it was very quiet outside.

Then, I turned to Ringo and said, "Everything will be okay."

Immediately after I spoke, we heard a loud VROOM from the military Jeep not too far away from where we were. The Jeep quickly passed alongside the canal.

"AH! We're never going to get out of here like this, Viorel. Let's face it, not with that stubborn Jeep hunting us down!" Ringo said a little too loudly.

The Jeep driver had a flashlight and pointed it down into the canal concrete floor, trying to locate us as cold dirt showered us.

Thankfully, we were pressed down so close to the other wall that we were out of his sight.

When the Jeep made its second trip against us, my heart felt like it was about to explode. I was so petrified; I could hardly think clearly or move my body. Suddenly, the Jeep drove away.

The next morning, we continued to make our way through the 100-acre cornfield. Thank God we survived through the four days and four nights there.

I felt like I'd been in this cornfield for over a month without food, shelter, or water, but it had only been four days. Time was dragging, and the four of us became weary and extremely tired. We were unable to sleep because we did not want to be seen.

We continued walking through the field, and to our surprise, we found blackberries in the field. We devoured them. The berries were so rich in flavor, unlike berries found in the food market. These berries had no preservatives and no GMO. They were 100% organic, large, and freshly grown. We kept eating them until we were completely satisfied. We also stuffed some extra berries in our pockets for later.

Shortly after that, I discovered fresh water in a ditch. The water was drinkable and crystal clear. I remember drinking that water; it tasted natural, and for a moment, I felt like I was in paradise.

I believe that Romania has the best natural groundwater in the world. We got down on the floor to drink the fresh water and then gasped for air afterward.

I began to thank God when I realized we had berries to eat and fresh water to drink. God was looking out for us! I couldn't have been more thankful.

As we continued walking, I told my friends that I had to take a short detour to empty my bladder. I went some distance away through the cornfield alone with the Holy Bible I had been carrying all this time. I stopped to pray and thank God for his protection and support. My heart became very thankful that I had made it this far without getting caught by the patrol officers.

I started expressing my thankfulness to God by singing songs to the Lord and reading my Bible. Then after about thirty minutes, I returned to my friends, and we continued our journey.

When I returned, my friends said, Be careful! We heard some voices in the distance. We need to be on the lookout. They were worried that it could have been the patrol officers. But those voices came from me the entire time while praying and singing to God out in the distance. When alone, I raised my voice louder and louder without being afraid of being caught. They were relieved when they realized it was me.

We were almost out of the cornfield and only minutes away from reaching the other side of the country. It was early morning, and the sun had already risen. A stillness rested on us. It was peaceful and quiet everywhere. All we heard was our own footsteps.

I told the guys, "We made it; we are just a few minutes away from reaching Serbia!"

We were walking, and I quietly and urgently said, "Hold on! Don't move! Get down!"

I noticed many soldiers far in the distance lying on the floor, sleeping. We were fortunate not to have stepped upon a soldier as we passed through the field, let alone during the night.

"This is too easy!" I said to my friends. I encouraged them to stay quiet and slowly walk through the field so the soldiers wouldn't hear us.

Giuca Voicu asked me, "What will you do once you arrive in America?"

"I'm going to start a new family and a new life in the land of the free," I replied.

The four of us began discussing our plans for when we arrived at our particular destination for freedom. Ringo wanted to go to Italy and stay there to escape from communism. I thought it would have been better to flee from Europe altogether.

We each wanted our own dream lifestyle, dream job, dream car, and dream house. We were very excited as we were about to cross into Serbia.

We were still about a mile away from crossing, but the corn stalks were making too much noise, so we had to slow down our walk and be more careful. Ringo was losing patience as we became tired and uneasy. I told him that slow is smooth and smooth is fast; eventually, we will get to the other side and that he should not worry.

Ringo began to grunt and sound irritated because he couldn't take this any longer. He completely lost his temper. He wouldn't stop complaining.

"What the hell is taking so long?! I am tired of staying in this cornfield!" Ringo said. "I just want to go to Yugoslavia and drink Coca-Cola in peace. I can't take this anymore."

"Shhh! Don't wake up the guards! Have you lost your mind, Ringo?" I replied.

In front of us, maybe a couple of hundred feet away, there were dozens of border patrol soldiers asleep on their bellies. Suddenly, a noise sounded from some distance. I became aghast as I turned to see where the noise was coming from. To my right, a mom deer stood up from the cornfield and began to cry with a very loud, bleating sound.

I felt my stomach drop. All the border patrol soldiers immediately jumped up and began grabbing their Avtomat Kalashnikov gas-operated assault rifles.

"What have you done, Ringo? You're going to have us killed!" I yelled.

We tried to run away, but one soldier summoned us to stop, saying loudly, "STATI!" Then he fired bullets in the sky to set off an alarm for other soldiers.

We knew we wouldn't get away alive, so we stopped running and did as the soldier commanded. The soldier told us to throw down our belongings and get down on the ground, so we did as he commanded.

Laying on our bellies with our arms and legs stretched out, we were shaking and breathing heavily on the dirt floor. Once the soldiers approached us, a soldier told us to locate the other runners who were associated with us, but it was only the four of us and no one else.

Instantly, several guards gathered around us and kicked and beat us severely. I was tossed and turned on the dirty corn stalk ground as the soldiers inflicted pain on my stomach, kidneys, entire back, shin, face, and throat. These men were ruthless; they did not care about my life or future.

This dream I had of fleeing Romania was a dream I had held onto since I was a little kid. The energy left in my body was taken away from me as they beat me nearly to death.

My vision became blurry after being in tears for so long. I saw many human figures above me, beating and laughing at my friends and me. Their motive was to beat us to death and leave us on the floor so they could eventually shoot us for fun or use us as human target practice.

I began to envision the life I had dreamt of for years. To start a new life in America and raise a new family in freedom so my kids could have a bright future.

I did not want to escape Romania for my own benefit. I wanted to start a new life for my future family, to be free from communism. There is more to life than living in a Soviet satellite country ruled by many inconsiderate dogs.

I saw a vision, a bright dream where I could work wherever I wanted and have a healthy family in America where we could make our own choices. As I imagined how it would be in America after fleeing, I instantly felt the worst pain in my life. SHH-HHUNK! A soldier stabbed me in my back near the spine with a bayonet. He knelt on top of me to tie my wrists together with his shoelace.

"Ahhhgh! I screamed as I felt the knife run three inches down my back. The soldier kept it in place for about thirty seconds before removing the knife from my flesh. I began to bleed severely, and they packed my wound with dirt.

They tied my wrists so tightly; my wrists and hands became numb. I could not feel anything other than the blood pulsing through my hands.

The soldier struggled to stand me up. My entire body became severely fatigued; I could not stand on my own two legs. My hair was messy and covered with dirt, as well as my face. My face looked weary and beat up, and I couldn't keep my eyes open. The border patrol soldier asked me how old I was. I was very short of breath. I began to stammer out my age with great effort. "Thir...thirt... thirty-three," I said. Then he spat on my mouth and pushed me onto the ground again.

I didn't feel anything because my adrenaline had not yet worn off. I overheard the other soldiers laughing and saying, Idiot. They scoffed at my friends and me.

The guards broke one of my friend's ribs while they beat him. It was such a scary and sad experience. We each saw our dream of fleeing Romania end right before our eyes.

I was lying on the ground with my hands tied behind my back, and the soldier stooped down to roll me over. I expected him to lift me again. Instead, he removed the bayonet and dug the tip of the rifle barrel deep into my mouth. He continued asking my friends and me if there were other men with us in our escape.

I nodded my head sideways as tears flowed down my face to confirm no one else was with us. The soldier did not believe us, so he applied more pressure down my mouth, which made me retch with a loud gagging sound.

"Hold it! This man cannot breathe! Are you out of your mind?" a fellow soldier exclaimed loudly.

The soldier continued to apply pressure with his barrel and whispered to me, "I can kill you at any time and leave you here to be eaten by the wild dogs! "

I looked into the eyes of the soldier with fear and a face full of tears. As I lay hopelessly on the dirty ground, void of enough breath in my lungs, I thought, "Will I ever go to America? Is this how it ends?

The images of my expectations after escaping Romania danced in my mind. I visualized the family I would have had in America, a life of freedom, a fresh start, free of communism and control. God forbid my children be born and raised here in Romanian, void of freedom and of choice.

The soldier took hold of my shirt and lifted me to my feet. The four of us were escorted by several soldiers to the Barack base. I asked for water.

"Water? Do you want water? Have some of this first!" The soldier behind me said, then he began to kick me from behind very hard, and he kicked my friends as well.

We asked them to stop, but they only abused us even harder. My friends and I were then escorted to the water fountain nearby for some water. After, the soldiers finally took us to the base for interrogation.

When I arrived at the Barack base, I was placed into a large room along with twenty other prisoners who were ready to be processed. A skinny, short doctor with a very thin mustache entered the room. He seemed very angry and in a rush. He told everyone to dress down so that we were all naked in the room and the doctor could proceed with the physical examination.

There was a mirror in front of me. I turned around and noticed the open wound on my back. That wound happened when the soldier accidentally stabbed me with his bayonet. I desperately sought medical attention from the doctor in the room, but he was very careless. He did not perform his duty professionally. He was only in it for easy money.

I was very frustrated because this communist doctor did not do his job, and I needed medical attention. He provided me with temporary medical attention and did not care to disinfect my wound. For all I knew, I could have been infected, and the doctor was very careless.

After the incomplete preliminary medical examination, I was taken into a small, dark interrogation room. A big, intimidating German shepherd in the room created an overwhelming atmosphere. I was told to remain standing during the entire interrogation session.

My feet were extremely sore and tired from my long journey through the cornfield. I couldn't stand the pain and agony. They asked who I was and why I was escaping. I told them I was fleeing for my freedom and no longer wanted anything to do with communist control. My response infuriated one of the soldiers. He partially let the German shepherd's leash loose to run very closely toward me. Then he caught the dog's leash just before it reached me.

Immediately, I felt a strong jolt looking at the dog's angry face and sharp wet teeth. The German shepherd began to bark at me very loudly and repeatedly. So much so that my Bible in my hands and my chest vibrated violently at every bark. Each bark startled me, and tears flowed down my face. I was terrified.

"Who is your ringleader," the interrogator shouted. I did not say a word. I kept quiet because I was afraid. The interrogator said that he would have the German shepherd bite me if I did not tell him who my ringleader was. I couldn't stop myself from shaking because these soldiers could easily let the dog bite me.

The soldiers were ruthless, beyond unorthodox, corrupt, and very unpredictable. I did not know what was going to happen next. It was a terrifying and hopeless moment. I did not know when the interrogation was going to end. That was the worst part of it all.

Then the interrogator stared at me for several seconds without saying a word. Suddenly I became very anxious that he would release the German shepherd. I bowed my head, and I looked down at the floor. I closed my eyes, and tears rolled down my cheeks.

I asked God for help. I needed him to rescue me because I had made it this far. There was no way it could possibly end here. I began to have flashbacks of when I gave my life to Jesus Christ. I also pondered on the time I was baptized at the First Baptist Church.

I still remember getting up from that seat and walking up to be baptized and submerged in water. I could still feel Jesus' peace in my heart, even as I sat before the angry interrogator.

It was my joy to express outwardly to the church congregation the inward decision I had made to follow Jesus Christ for all my days. When I was at the First Baptist Church a while ago, I was standing in the water tub with my pastor as he was speaking.

I was then submerged in water and then lifted. As I was raised from the water, I felt like a new person. I began laughing as I felt so much joy in my heart. My face was wet. I had my eyes closed because of the water. My pastor lifted my arm towards the roof as many of the congregants celebrated loudly in joy and began applauding.

I was full of joy and tears that day. I will never forget the things Jesus did in my life. I was thankful that I made it this far. However, I didn't think I could move on because my life may be over.

"WAKE UP! Did I say you can sleep?" The interrogator yelled as he forcefully struck my shin with his boot. My flashback was greatly interrupted, and I immediately lifted my head and looked at the interrogator.

Then a chief commander approached me with a clipboard, paper, and pencil. He instructed me to write a declaration about everything that had happened in the cornfield and how I got there. I slowly took hold of the clipboard with a clumsy grip. The clipboard fell on the floor.

The chief was furious and struck me several times with his baton. The chief did not know that my arms and hands were completely numb and shaky after being tied up for so long with the shoelace.

I took the clipboard again and tried writing, but my hands were numb and shaking uncontrollably. I was unable to write, no matter how hard I tried.

The chief had no mercy. He continued to strike my buttocks and call me names. One of the soldiers told the chief to stop and let me rest for a few minutes.

The soldiers noticed I was the only one in the group with a Holy Bible. The interrogator looked down at the Bible, then looked at me, and said with a scowl," Read something to me!

I picked up my Bible and turned to a random page. My hands were sweaty and shaky. The page opened to Acts chapter 17, verses 30 and 31. I read the scriptures to the interrogator as tear drops landed on the scripture I was reading. The scripture read: God overlooked such ignorance in the past, but now he commands all people everywhere to repent. For he has set a day when he will judge the world with justice by the man he has appointed.

I looked toward the officer, and he said, "Now, sing a Christian song."

The interrogation room had dim lighting. It was very quiet, but they wanted to hear my song. I began to sing quietly with my soft, trembling voice. As I sang, I gained strength, and my voice became louder with more confidence. The interrogator standing before me with his angry German Shepherd began staring at me intently and curiously.

I think he realized how passionate I was about my faith in Jesus Christ, even during terror and uncertainty.

A chef in the kitchen across the room had observed everything that had happened from a distance. He felt compassion for me because I was brave for my faith. He approached me closely and quietly whispered in my ear, "Buddy, keep your faith. Do not let anyone dim your light. Come with me."

His words cheered me up, and the soldiers allowed me to go into the kitchen with the chef. I walked into the kitchen, and my jaw dropped. I saw plenty of food. The chef offered me a seat and a warm bowl of bean soup. As I sat down and looked around the kitchen, I began to thank God for rescuing me from hunger because I was starving. I was on my feet for days, and I had eaten nothing.

I was thankful because I was not supposed to be here right now. I should have been killed in the interrogation room. "Why is the chef so nice to me? Is this a set-up or a trap?" I asked myself. I was not sure. All I knew was that God protected me, and I was willing to continue trusting Him with my life.

I helped myself to the delicious soup in front of me. Then, I turned around and looked through the window, only to find the rest of my friends working. I was astounded to see my three other friends outside emptying the septic tank and cutting logs for fire use in the kitchen. I asked the chef, "Why am I here? Why are the others working outside?"

The chef replied, "I have seen how dedicated you were to your faith. You don't deserve to be treated that way by the soldiers."

I was perplexed, but I knew everything would be okay.

After I ate my meal, I was taken down to the basement where they had a prison cell hallway. The hallway guards were very discourteous and careless. They seldom would not allow me to use the hallway restroom. Even if they did, they told me to hurry up because they prioritized the bathroom for themselves.

When it was time for all the inmates to have our meals, a guard came to us, one cell at a time down the hallway, to serve us tea and stale bread. We all had our metal mugs ready.

When it was my turn to receive my meal, the guard approached my cell, handed me my stale bread, and asked for my mug so that the guard may fill it with tea. I extended my arm with the mug in my hand so that he may take it. He had no way of gripping the mug because I was holding onto the handle.

This guard quickly became agitated. In his rage, he took my metal mug, which was very heavy and dense, and attempted to throw it at me with full force. Luckily, he missed.

I was petrified and fell to the floor. The guard became angry only because he could not grip the mug's handle. I became heated as my heart rate went up. Thank God he missed me. Otherwise, I could have been seriously injured. I became very miserable because I knew I had to spend the next ten days here in this horrible place with poor conditions for quarantine.

After the ten days were up, we were transported to a prison site where I was placed in the middle of a dorm to join many crooks and horrible criminals for another ten days. I did nothing wrong. I was only here to flee for freedom and live a better life away from this country.

Many of the prisoners in my dorm began calling me a TRAITOR at the top of their lungs. I couldn't stand joining them in this prison dorm. I tried yelling at the guards to let me out and put me in another cell, but the guards just laughed and mocked me.

I was afraid the prisoners would attack me and kill me. I feared for my life. I was confused because I did not deserve to be in prison. It did not feel like prison; it felt like I was only visiting. But here I was, in the middle of the dorm, constantly mocked and ridiculed by inmates and guards for trying to flee this country.

Suddenly, with eyes wide open, I was mind-boggled. I remembered that I had brought my Holy Bible with me. I was blessed it wasn't confiscated because the officers would take it away, rip it apart, and use it as toilet paper.

I took my Holy Bible from my bunk bed and held it in my hands. I stared at this Holy Bible and took deep breaths with my eyes closed. Some inmates laughed at me, saying, "Hey, Mr. Fortune teller, tell me something I don't know."

I was standing in the middle of the cell where many inmates could see me, and the inmates only got louder and louder. They laughed at me while I held my Holy Bible.

With my eyes closed, I began remembering everything Jesus Christ had done for me thus far. I emptied my mind and pondered only on the Lord and who he was to me. I knew he wouldn't give up on me, as the Bible teaches.

Five minutes passed, and tears started to run down my face. Many inmates made fun of me and mocked me, saying, "Oh look, he's telling his own future!"

I opened my eyes and began to share the true gospel of Jesus Christ with all of them with love and compassion, with a loud and authoritative voice. I knew that my experience with Jesus Christ was real and powerful, so I expressed this passion to the inmates so they may have hope of salvation.

About an hour later, I still preached to the inmates that Jesus Christ came to earth two thousand years ago to live a perfect life that we could have never lived on our own. I also mentioned that He sacrificed his perfect innocent life and died in our place on the cross, that Jesus himself may take our condemnation of hell away from us, and that we may be free.

The cells became very quiet as all the inmates listened intently to every word I spoke. The words I said were God's true, everlasting, living Word. The inmates were interested because that was something their souls needed to hear. Some were crying and sobbing. I continued to preach repentance and God's everlasting kindness and love. I did not stop. I knew God was in that cell with me just as He was with Daniel in the lion's den because the atmosphere changed. The atmosphere went from a place of violence and rage to a place of peace and love. It was the strangest and most exciting experience I have ever had.

God was taking over. He did his work in this prison. Even the guards listened as I preached. Nothing could stop the Word of God from being preached. One inmate had tears flowing down his cheeks. He told me that as soon as he left this prison, he would convert to Christianity. I mentioned he could convert right where he was standing. Right now.

Many more inmates stood up, wiped their faces, and talked to me. Many inmates wanted to convert to Jesus Christ in the cell where I was standing. I was overwhelmed by this, and I had the confidence to lead them into a prayer. I also instructed them on how to live a Christian life and told them how much Jesus Christ loved them. Many were joyful and praised God for what had just happened.

I found this very hard to believe because not too long ago, I was physically and verbally threatened by these inmates, and now, many of them were new believers in a matter of a few hours. Praise God, Praise God, I shouted.

After some time, the prison administration decided to relocate my other inmates and me into a much larger cell that could fit about sixty people.

There were many rows of three-level bunk beds in this cell. I had the very top bunk. The ceiling was only three feet away from my face, so it was difficult for me to maneuver. I had difficulty sleeping because there was multiple linear lighting across the ceiling, one right above my face. I couldn't sleep, no matter how hard I tried. I wish I could've turned off the linear ceiling lights, but the guards did not allow me to shut off the lights due to surveillance and safety reasons.

I also had to stay up late some nights to protect myself from inmates who were gay sex violators, and that only made my nights worse. The living conditions were terrible, and no one cared about you in this cell.

Many inmates surrendered their lives to Christ, but some were still careless, and the guards became more ruthless and reckless every day. The sleeping conditions were one of the worst experiences I've had. I would wake up feeling worse than I did the day before.

My shift was about to begin. The hallway patrol guard instructed us to go on a rotating shift. One inmate would stay up through the night for about two hours and 45 minutes to patrol my large cell. The cell was about 350 square feet, and I was the first inmate to begin this rotating shift. I was commanded to stand throughout the shift and patrol across the rows of bunk beds to ensure everyone was sleeping and safe. I was not allowed to wear a watch during my shift. Only the guard would let me know when my shift was over.

It was inconvenient, but it made the time go by much faster. Every time a new inmate started his shift, he was asked to wash the dorm floor with his bare hands, using a wet rug. As for me, I was given the chore of cleaning the entire dorm floor. I had to reach under the bunk beds to wipe clean under the beds. I couldn't help but gag when I saw some disgusting trash under the beds. It was horrible.

Overall, the living experience at this prison was abysmal. I had very little sleep because of my shift. No one cared about you, and the entire prison smelled disgusting. I wish for no one to experience this living condition, but I came to this prison to fight for my freedom. I was brave enough to take this risk, and I do not regret it.

One night when we all went to sleep, I had an unusual dream, one I had never had before. I dreamt that many of my inmates jumped out the windows and fled this prison. I was confused as I looked around in my dream.

Everyone was in a rush. Everything was happening so fast; I couldn't keep up. I looked up at the clock on the wall, and its arms rapidly spun uncontrollably. Instantly, I awoke and sat straight up with eyes wide open, feeling disoriented. I didn't understand what had happened because that dream felt so real.

I looked around the prison dorm and saw many of my inmates looking through the prison window overseeing downtown Timișoara, called Popa Șapcă.

Some Gypsies were loudly playing their accordions and other musical instruments on the main street sidewalks. I asked one of my inmates what was going on outside.

"You haven't heard?" he replied. He said President Nicolae Ceausescu issued an amnesty for all men and women who exercised their rights to flee Romania and other similar crimes. The amnesty does not apply to people who committed bribes and corruption. They are not eligible. I felt very sorry for many Christians who committed bribery to get hold of new Bibles and other materials because they were not permitted this amnesty.

One week later, I was released from prison because President Nicolae Ceausescu issued an amnesty for me. This was such a huge price to pay after trying to flee Romania. My mother, Minca, was waiting for me outside by the prison gates to see me for the first time in a long time.

My father was also supposed to come to see me during this visitation, but only one visitor was allowed, so my mom came alone. She seemed older than before, having gray hair and some extra wrinkles on her face, but my mother was still beautiful.

She offered me a bag of edible refreshments and a cigarette. I refused the cigarette because I was a Christian and did not want to smoke. She loved how I transformed into a better man and was filled with the Holy Spirit inside of me. I told her about my entire experience in prison and how God used me to lead many people to Christ's salvation.

Minca was very surprised, and she was proud of me. I became a huge inspiration to my mother as she did not know Christ personally. When Minca heard my story, she decided to become more serious about following Jesus and also chose to surrender her life to follow Jesus. This was an amazing experience for her, and for me, as our friendship was so strong. When I grew up as a kid, she knew of God, and we read various Bible verses, but she did not know Jesus at a personal level. Now that she is, from this time forward, she deepened her friendship and understanding of who Jesus is.

Now that I remember, I was in that prison for over two months or more, and that dream rang a bell. I was supposed to be in this prison for almost three years, but I was there for less than three months. That dream about the clock arms spinning very fast was a sign from God that I would be released from prison earlier than intended. Praise God. I was very thankful that President Ceausescu allowed amnesty for other prisoners and me.

Once I left the prison site, I returned to my apartment, which my job provided me while working as a lathe operator at the Uzina Mecanica Timișoara (UMT). I began praying and asking God that Human Resources would allow me to keep this apartment even after I left this job.

The UMT provided equipment and tools for me to use while working for them, and they were generous in giving married couples an apartment to stay in while working for them. It was a great perk. As I mentioned, I was divorced from my ex-wife, but I did not have the court issue my divorce papers, so the UMT thought I was still married. That was why I had this apartment because only married employees or employees with kids were allowed to have this amazing benefit. That was why I prayed and fasted that I may keep this apartment even after quitting this job. I begged God that he would make a way because I wanted to start a family in the future, and I needed this apartment.

I went to the UMT factory where I was working and let them know I was quitting. They instructed me to pick up a list of instructions and surrender all my working equipment and tools in my work area cabinet. My manager wanted to ensure that I brought everything near my workstation back to the equipment department, where all parts and tools were stored. I left my workstation area clean as I was very organized and clean as usual.

I had checked off everything on my list that I needed to surrender. Now, the Human Resources office was just around the corner where I needed to go so that the officer could check off the remainder of the list, which was the apartment I also had to surrender. My hands began to sweat, and I became very nervous. I knew the officer would check my list. I did not want the officer to check off the apartment because I really needed it. I had been praying for days that I could keep this apartment, that God would make a way for me and leave that box unchecked.

Before I walked into that HR office, I began praying in the hallway for about thirty minutes, begging God to hear my cry. Only God knows how much I needed this apartment. It wasn't easy to get an apartment in those days, and I did not want to lose it.

As my hands were sweating and shaking, I sighed while making my way into the HR office. I had the officer read through everything he needed to check off the list. He made sure I returned all the tools and equipment. After ten minutes of checking everything off the list, he handed my list back to me.

I couldn't believe what had just happened next. I was completely amazed and in awe of how big my God is. The officer forgot to check my apartment off my list. I did not have to give up my stay at that apartment. I continued to pray and fast for days after HR signed my paper. I wanted to make sure HR did not return to me and take my apartment away. I was extremely thankful to God that he answered my prayer. God is real and was working in my life to protect me.

Fleeing from Romania, 1987

I entered a new season of fasting and prayer. I set out on a mission to find my wife now that I am out of prison, and I would attempt to flee Romania once again.

8

FINDING THE LOVE OF MY LIFE, 1988

Since I left my former job at the UMT, I had the apartment all to myself and plenty of time on my hands. I began to attend church and join in prayer with my Christian friends so I could branch out and come closer to my creator.

- On Mondays, I attended a youth Bible study at Pentecostal Church in Timișoara called Elim on Romulus Street.
- On Tuesdays, I attended youth Bible study at the First Baptist Church, now called Bethel, on the same street.
- On Wednesdays, I attended morning, afternoon, and evening prayer meetings at different friends' homes, which was nice because it was also a potluck night. Because I was single, I enjoyed attending prayer night/potlucks because I did not cook much at my apartment. I enjoyed eating together with my godly friends.

- On Thursdays, I attended the Pentecostal Church service at Elim.
- And on Fridays, I attended First Baptist Church services.
- Then on Saturdays, I went to Adventist Church.
- On Sundays, I attended First Baptist Church in the mornings and evenings.

I felt compelled to seek God with all my heart by fasting, praying everyday, and eating only at night because I was hungry for God's presence. I also wanted to expedite my answer to prayer on finding my true wife, the love of my life.

I went to a prayer meeting one evening in August 1988 and stumbled across someone I hadn't seen in 14 years, Victor Marian. He was an excellent painter and carpenter and one of the humblest souls you could ever know. He and I met before, but suddenly he vanished, and I never saw him again until now, which was very fortunate for me because he has become one of my greatest friends.

One night after prayer, as our gathering was over, we talked for a while, and I invited him to stay the night at my apartment in Timișoara. During his stay, we fixed some food and discussed our experiences in Romania during the communist regime. We also had Bible discussions and talked about God. We were both believers.

We had great conversations and heartbreaking conversations, too. None of our stories were good. We both had terrible experiences due to the regime. We devised a plan to leave the country for the second time and go to Yugoslavia, now called Serbia and Montenegro (since the early 1990s).

I told him my horrible story of being captured near the border, and we put together some solutions for a successful escape.

It is not easy to flee Romania. We knew many people took these chances, and they never saw another day. Victor and I were brave enough to try to escape because we knew a better life awaited us in America.

The following day, we took a train to Buziaş, and he invited me to his house. He introduced me to his wife, Rebecca. They were both sweet people, full of love and caring hearts. Rebecca recommended I visit often and stay as long as I need to, at least until I find myself a wife and get situated with my own family. I wanted to have a wife and a child before leaving this country to have a head start and have my own family.

I occasionally rode my bike to Victor's house to talk and stay the night. We became very good friends. In September 1988, I went to visit Victor and Rebecca. Victor and I walked to his backyard to clean his car, the beetle he had parked in his backyard. He eventually paid me one hundred lei.

As we were talking, someone caught my eye. As I turned and looked at Rebecca. I did a double take of someone whom I had never met before. She was gorgeous. She had long black hair with a beautiful smile. As I stared at her, trying to eavesdrop, I was also trying to keep up with what Victor was saying.

His voice became indistinct and unclear as I paid more attention to Rebecca and this girl.

"Do you agree?" asked Victor

"Agree with what?" Victor noticed I was not paying attention. He stood up to see what I was looking at and assumed I was interested in this new girl in the kitchen. He explained who she was and told me her name.

Georgeta Marian. I did not meet her because I was too shy. From a distance, she seemed to look like a very gentle-spirited person. I left Victor's backyard and entered the kitchen, where Georgeta and Rebecca conversed. I sat on the kitchen stool,

Finding the Love of My Life, 1988

waiting to eat something, and Rebecca introduced me to Georgeta. She was so sweet and considerate.

My first impression of her was breathtaking because she was not only beautiful, but she had a higher level of hospitality than anyone I had ever known. Georgeta also seemed to be a hard worker and extremely determined when in the kitchen. The kitchen was her happy place. I saw her pounding away against the dough-filled mixing bowl and mastering her task of making the best plum dumplings known to humankind.

She was very attentive to her work. She spread the dough, placed the plums in it, and rolled them. She was fast. I was amazed at her cooking skills. She was fast and precise, and she managed her time well when cooking.

I was attracted to Georgeta because she was very humble and a hard worker. I had the privilege of trying the plum dumplings she had made. I felt like I was sitting on an island. I could taste every flavor so clearly and then follow the aftertaste, which was fantastic. *Who is this woman?*, I thought to myself. Georgeta was too good to be true.

I was extremely nervous and did not engage in a conversation with Georgeta. After Georgeta left the house, Rebecca turned to me and said that perhaps I could marry Georgeta. I assumed she was taken by now. After all, she was too good to be true.

"Nonsense, she is single," Rebecca confirmed. She was determined to help me form a relationship with Georgeta because I was not married and lived alone.

For the longest time, Georgeta seemed like a beautiful mystery. She seemed to have everything I ever wanted in a woman, but she never said a word. I would often ride my bicycle to Rebecca's house. Sometimes Georgeta would be there cooking and talking to Rebecca.

One day as I commuted home on my bike, I had a flashback of a week before meeting Georgeta for the first time. I remembered leaving a church service and then traveling to my parent's house for lunch. I passed through a neighborhood where I encountered a group of kids playing volleyball on the street in front of their homes.

I remembered seeing Georgeta on the front yard playing volleyball with whom I perceived to be her sisters and brothers because many of them looked alike. But now that I was introduced to Georgeta, it made more sense. That was her all along, playing volleyball and being athletic. That flashback surprised me; I was willing to visit her home one day and say hello.

I continued to fast and pray for many days that God could guide me in finding my wife, perhaps, Georgeta. From time to time, I ran across George's father, Georghia Marian, at a Pentecostal church in Buziaș. He also saw me bike through his neighborhood almost every day. Eventually, we had a conversation. He invited me to his place for lunch.

I accepted his invitation. I was thrilled to visit his home and see Georgeta again, perhaps even talk to her. I walked into his home and was overwhelmed by the number of girls living in this house. So many things were happening. Girls walked across the hallway, entering one room and exiting from the other. It was a bustling home. I was baffled because there were so many girls. I did not know which one was Georgeta because many looked alike.

I spotted Georgeta in her happy place, the kitchen. If I ever needed to find Georgeta, the kitchen was the only place to find her.

Georghia Marian announced we would have chicken soup for lunch. So, we sat at the dining table and had an interesting conversation about scripture and life. He went on and on about scripture. I cannot recall exactly what he talked about because I was so caught up in what Georgeta was doing in the kitchen. I would hear Georghia Marian talking, but I focused on Georgeta killing it in the kitchen.

She would approach our table, serve us and then walk back to the kitchen. Georghia would tell me that Georgeta made these foods and how talented she was.

When will I get to talk to her? Yet again, she would approach our table, hand us another course, take my dirty dishes and walk away without saying a word. I want to meet and pursue this girl, I thought to myself. Georghia continued to brag about Georgeta and say that out of fourteen siblings, she was the one who held down the kitchen fort.

I was amazed at her excellence and attention to detail. Even though I had never had a conversation with her, I was attracted to her work ethic. That made her even more beautiful.

After some time, Georghia and the rest of Georgeta's siblings went to their rooms, and only Georgeta and I were in the kitchen. She was working very hard, trying to wash the dishes. Then, she looked back at me, and I was very nervous.

When she saw me, she looked as though she felt bad for me. After all, I was very skinny and tired. I did not always wear very nice clothes.

Georghia invited me to his home for lunch every so often, and I eventually developed the courage to spark some neat conversations with Georgeta. I became comfortable talking to her because I had frequently visited her home.

Georgia enjoyed my company, and things started to go very well for me regarding getting to know Georgeta and her family. Soon after, with Rebecca's help, Georgeta, Rebecca, and I planned a trip to Timișoara. We took the train there. The three of us stopped by my apartment, and I gave them a tour. Georgeta and I had been talking for some time, and I had been fasting for quite some time. Georgeta had also been fasting and praying to seek a lovely, god-fearing man of God as her husband. Georgeta seemed quite interested in how clean my apartment was. Everything was spotless and organized.

I had painted the walls and bought new furniture; I had all I needed only to find my wife. Georgeta noticed how I loved to cook and prepare my meals.

The three of us hung out in the apartment. We also went on short walks around town and had a great time. Georgeta, Rebecca, and I went on more fun trips together as we enjoyed each other's company. We went to visit some prophets and to speak to them. They would prophesy over us. It was an amazing experience.

In October 1988, Georgeta sought the Lord Jesus. She had a positive dream about me being her husband. She did not care what anyone thought about her decision. she knew it was the Lord telling her to make this decision. That decision was to go to her home Pentecostal church in Buziaş and consult her pastor, Pastor Leontiuc, about potentially marrying me. I also consulted my pastor, Pastor Dugulescu, at First Baptist Church in Timişoara about marrying Georgeta.

Things started to progress so fast. Georgeta and I had met in early October, and we had planned to get married sometime in late November. Her siblings were surprised that she had moved so quickly.

After consecutively visiting Georgeta and her family, I'd learned what her family was like and how honest she was.

At this point, Georgeta and I had been going on consistent romantic date nights, and I called her Geta for the first time. Some of our best date nights consisted of going on long walks and listening to each other's stories. We walked to a fine restaurant one day. Geta was kind enough to buy my meal, and we both had chicken soup, one of the best soups we've ever had.

One date night, in particular, we were walking on the sidewalk. Geta was walking next to me to my right, where the sidewalk cuts off and meets with the road. I was nervous for Geta because I didn't want her to be closer to oncoming traffic, so I had her switch spots with me so that I was walking near the edge of the sidewalk. I cared for her safety because the Bible says in Ephesians 5:28 that a man who loves a woman shows love for himself.

Only a couple of months had passed since Geta and I had our first official conversation. It was time to prepare for our wedding ceremony, which was set for November 26, 1988.

I was very responsible with my finances, so I had been saving some extra cash to fund our wedding ceremony.

In 1988 there was a food shortage in Romania because of poor economic management made by the nation's president in the 1970s, which led to massive foreign debt. This meant exporting many goods, such as food, to other countries, which Romania needed to pay back. This also meant that we were very short on food for the wedding day, which placed an extra burden on Geta and me.

Dr. Nicolae Chera, a veterinarian at the Communist State Farm, had the only solution I needed to fix this problem. He has plenty of food given to him by the government to supply food for local stores and to the cows and horses on the State Farm. So, I visited Dr. Nicolae and asked if he could provide us with one liter of thin, sweet-sour cream, which we desperately needed to make our wedding cake. All the stores were out of thin sweet-sour cream.

He said he could not make any promises but would try to provide us with that thin sweet-sour cream. Not too long after, he stopped by Geta's house because he knew Geta and her family. He gave Geta two liters of the sour cream I had asked for, which was all for free.

This was a big blessing from God because he is providing for us. Liviu Radu also brought chickens from another county in Buziaș Hunedoara. Liviu had many special connections with people across Buziaș. He could ask around and receive help from others at any time.

From these chickens, we made chicken noodle soup, cabbage rolls, schnitzel, mashed potatoes, roasted chicken, and plenty more foods. Marian Elena did not believe that there would be enough food to supply so many people, so we only invited nearly one hundred of our closest family and friends within the area. Most of our guests came from our church, Pentecost Church of Buziaș.

I purchased my very own tailored, beige suit to wear at the wedding, which was only one day away. Let me just say, I was quite nervous about this wedding. Walking in south Timișoara, I was on my way to Buziaș, where the wedding would take place the following day. I was in Timișoara to quickly prepare myself for the wedding and head back to Buziaș again. I carried a duffel bag over my shoulders containing the flower bouquet, my custom suit, and other essential wedding materials.

Ten angry, loose dogs randomly ran toward me and began to encircle me. I was traumatized and confused at the same time. I was not about to get eaten alive by some while dogs, especially before my wedding day. I swung my bag around towards the dogs to scare them away. They were not afraid of my duffel bag. In fact, one of the dogs latched its sharp teeth onto my bag and would not let go. This dog was destroying my bag, and other dogs were getting closer to me and barking loudly. Eventually, the dog let go, and I kept swinging my bag around. The dogs were very stubborn and did their best to continue attacking me.

I was sweating and frightened because I did not want to die this evening. I started yelling very loudly to scare them off. Finally, they ran off and never came back. What an experience, I almost lost my life.

I survived, and finally, the big day arrived. The ceremony occurred at the Pentecost Church of Buziaș in the late evening. I walked in with my beige suit, waiting for my bride to arrive. My hands began sweating, and I needed to sit down for a while during the ceremony. I was too nervous to stand up. I wanted the ceremony to end already because my body temperature was rising due to the stress levels I was experiencing. A minute felt like an hour to me.

But through it all, I enjoyed every moment as there will only be one wedding ceremony for Georgeta and me. As the ceremony began to wrap up, we did not exchange rings because we did not feel the need to have them for our marriage. We did not believe in wearing a physical ring on our ring fingers as many people do to symbolize commitment, love, and devotion. We believed our hearts for one another served as a better token than just having a physical ring on our physical fingers. Funny to say, but this idea also lowered our wedding budget.

Once the ceremony ended, many of our guests cheered and commemorated our wedding with loud shouts of celebration. We noticed people began to leave the church to move to the reception. It was already dark outside, and a violent rainstorm shook the church building.

As they departed, they congratulated us. This was honestly the best time for both of us. We felt welcomed, and a few special people came to talk to us before going to the reception. We both felt very blessed, and my heart was full of joy.

Just when I thought it couldn't get any better, Geta and I were in the back, talking to a couple of people. Most people had already left the church. We walked to the front of the church and found everyone had left, including our band and transportation. Geta's brother was our designated driver, but he left without us. I guess he was hungry.

The only people left in the church were a couple of kids playing and running around in the back with their guardians. Hearing the kids play and screams echo across the walls in an empty church during a stormy and rainy night was such a bummer.

"Vio, they forgot about us. We were the only ones here!" Geta said with a look of concern on her face.

We thought about walking, but that was impossible with the heavy rainstorm outside. So, we called a friend to quickly come and pick us up before there was no more food left for us.

When we finally made our grand entrance to the reception, everyone just ate and focused on their plate in front of them. All our guests were seated along a forty-five-foot-long table that stretched across the entire home where the reception took place in Buziaș.

We had all the food we needed thanks to Liviu Radu and many other people who had helped. Despite our transportation from the ceremony to the reception, this was an amazing time. I was very blessed to marry the love of my life, Geta Matei. She was my world, and I couldn't wait to experience life with her.

After Geta and I married, we had our honeymoon at my apartment in Timișoara; not the flashiest vacation, but it fitted us. We spent quality time together and did not work for almost three months, thanks to those who gifted us with wedding money.

Finding the Love of My Life, 1988

A couple of Geta's sisters gifted us one hundred de lei each, Romanian currency. With one hundred de lei, we could stay home without work for three months, no problem.

Geta was a very thoughtful soul. She loved being on her feet. The minute she moved into my apartment, she began operating the kitchen and cooking many pastries and food. I was not allowed to step foot into the kitchen because I was no longer in charge of the kitchen.

Cozonac, a sweetened, flaky bread, began piling up on the counters in large sums. Romanian dessert salami and filled peach cookies covered the entire dining tabletop. After finishing my short nap, I woke up to a house overflowing with pastries. I saw Geta's hands still at work after hours had passed. The kitchen was her happy place.

She never overworked herself; cooking was her way of relaxing and charging up. I was blessed to have her in my life. When we finished our honeymoon, I began working again, delivering food from warehouses and supplying local grocery stores. I drove a white van around town to earn an honest dollar. I came home with boxes full of fresh, free food.

It was quite exciting and fulfilling to work hard for an honest pay. I desired to provide for my family, and I enjoyed doing so.

After months of Geta and I spending quality time and getting to know each other for quite some time, we decided to expand our family. We asked God for healthy children because that was what we wanted.

In mid-January 1989, we received medical reports from our doctor that Geta was pregnant with our first baby. My heart was filled with joy. I was truly at a loss for words. I felt too young for this. It seemed too soon to be true.

Then, on September 18, 1989, Geta gave birth to our first baby girl, Priscila Gabriela Matei. Nothing brings you greater joy than seeing your baby face-to-face. This girl brightened my life, and every day became better and better. I felt blessed. I knew that Jesus Christ was at the center of our family. Knowing that I have a child under my roof made me more determined to provide and move to America, where freedom awaits us.

During the summer of 1989, I went to the U.S embassy to apply for a VISA card. I went to apply because Geta heard from her sister that anyone who suffered time in prison for freedom would receive an easy access to a VISA card. The U.S embassy was doing this for political reasons like asylum. So, I paid a visit to the embassy located in Bucharest.

I spent an entire day waiting in line to get into the embassy. I finally arrived at the location but could not walk in because the counselor was not in the office. I walked in after hours. That was a difficult moment for me. I had no shelter and no place to stay for the night. I needed a place to lay my head. I was disappointed because I needed this VISA as soon as possible to take my family to America and fulfill my God-given dream.

Even though I was disappointed, I was not discouraged. I never give up. A failure is an opportunity if you choose not to give up and instead move forward. I tried my best to find a safe place to rest amidst the dangerous revolution.

I traveled for hours trying to find a place to sleep. My mind was getting ready to shut down because my body needed sleep. I eventually found a train station in Bucharest. They had benches and chairs where I could rest. However, this was extremely risky because everyone was required to show proof of identification that you are employed. Officers patrolled the train station, and those with no job and no ID could be sent to prison.

Finding the Love of My Life, 1988

I did not want to return to prison, so I had to hide from the officers constantly looking for suspects.

I found a bench hidden behind a pillar just across the railroad tracks in the subway. I was exhausted and couldn't help but fall asleep to the rumbling ambiance the train made. It was a constant white noise.

I mistakenly fell asleep in a sitting position with my head bowed sideways and my hands in each pocket to secure the five hundred lei Romanian money I possessed. Unaware of my surroundings, I was vulnerable to potential threats because I was asleep.

Numerous crimes occurred in these train stations, and I was the only man asleep during that time. Suddenly, two men approached while I was in my deep sleep. They sat next to me on either side. They desperately needed money. They knew I was sleeping and saw that I protected both pockets. They knew I was hiding something. The man on my right assumed I had money, so he carefully pulled my hand out of my pocket. But just before he reached his hand to take my money, I was startled out of my deep sleep and yelled at them to leave me alone.

They took off suddenly and never came back. I checked my pockets. I still had all my money. I was thankful to God that he woke me up just in time. Praise God! They almost took my VISA money from me. That would have been a bad day for my family and me.

At 6:30 a.m., I made my way to the U.S embassy for the second time, hoping that I could finally get what I needed from them. I picked up a waiting ticket. I was number eight hundred. I waited for hours until my number was called.

This is life in Romania. It was 2 p.m. and I eventually walked into a security checking station. Two security guards stopped me and asked me why I was there. I told them that I was imprisoned and tortured for seeking freedom.

Then after the security check, they let me through, and I could have never been happier than I was at that moment. Thank God, I made it through that security station. My heart was pounding, thinking that I would not make it. I was then given a form with VISA instructions. I filled it out and turned it in. Then I sat in the lobby and waited for my name to be called. After a while, the agent at the counsel desk called me up and asked why I was there, while he looked through my forms.

I told the agent I was there to get my VISA and leave the country. He told me I could not leave the country because I wasn't qualified. I had no idea what that meant. I was disappointed, especially with having my second daughter on the way. I wanted to start a new life in America. This cannot be happening. The agent knew that I was imprisoned for trying to flee the country. I finished up with the agent and traveled back home. I was disappointed. The security guards let me in. I didn't understand the rest.

One month after I applied for my Visa, I still hoped to hear back from the U.S embassy. I was disappointed but not discouraged. Giving up was not an option. I put in the work, and I already paid the price to leave the country. I attempted to flee, but instead, I was imprisoned.

Just when you think you made it, life happens, dragging you down again. Life is unpredictable, and I had to learn to adapt to the downfalls.

My mind was a mess for weeks because I overthought whether the U.S embassy accepted me or not. So, I prayed and asked God for wisdom.

After praying, I needed to spend quality time with my family and care for them. After all, that was my role as a father. I learned to be present at the moment and focus on the task at hand. Worrying about the future was out of my control.

I knew that God had heard my prayer. I gave him my worries and prioritized my family's needs over mine. I've learned to give my request to God, then help others in the meantime.

God is great because I asked him for wisdom, and he answered my prayers by helping me love my family. As a result, He gave me what my heart desired—a VISA card.

I thought it was too late and the embassy wouldn't call back, but God had a plan. The U.S embassy called me days later and told me I was accepted and invited for an interview. I couldn't believe the news.

My dream came true. Years of hard work and prayer paid off. All glory to God. This was my chance to prove to many people all around the world that dreams can become a reality if you trust God and put in the hard work.

I was convinced that I would have a healthy family in America. My kids would live in freedom and have successful lives. I attended multiple interviews at the embassy, but I was approved. I am blessed and thankful. Ever since I was a kid, I wanted to catch a plane to America and seek freedom. Now it was happening. God is good, and this was all worth the hard work.

Although I was the happiest man alive, I had to keep away from the secret service officers, who had been watching me for quite some time.

9

THE ROMANIAN REVOLUTION, 1989

On December 15, 1989, a Revival gathering occurred at my local church in Timișoara. I traveled by bicycle to that gathering. My experience at the revival was amazing because I knew the Lord was there.

I reunited with some of my friends, and we understood that the real definition of revival was "a hungry heart for the Lord."
It seemed to be a normal night. I prayed at church, spent time with friends, and returned home to my wife. It was dark outside, and I rode my bike over wet roads after it rained a few hours prior to me leaving the church.

Suddenly, I heard the sound of wet tires from a car quickly approaching from behind and it hit me. The impact threw me sixteen feet into the oncoming traffic lane.

I was disoriented. I had muffled hearing and blurry vision, unsure of what had just happened. I lay in the middle of the wet road and saw what appeared to be two human figures standing over me, lifting me up. I couldn't see or hear well. I heard indistinct chatter from the two men helping me into their car.

A lady stood in front of her house and witnessed everything that had happened. She took my broken bicycle and shoes and stored them safely for me to retrieve later.

Honestly, if that lady did not witness this accident, the men who hit me would have driven off and left me on the road. Instead, they saw women looking at the scene, and the men drove me to the nearest hospital. I couldn't feel or move my left leg.

This worried me because I needed to support my wife and daughter. I wouldn't be able to work if something major had happened to my left leg.

When I arrived at the hospital, the doctors seemed disinterested in seeing me. They looked irritated. One of the doctors asked me why I bothered to come to the hospital. They were extremely rude to me.

I explained what had happened, and they were angry because I had given them a job to do. The doctors were very selfish and lazy. They did not care about their patients. They took their sweet time.

The x-rays revealed that my left leg was broken, fractured from my knee down to my upper ankle. There was no orthopedic surgeon in this hospital, so they took me by ambulance to an orthopedic hospital to place a cast on my leg. They put me on a plain, old gurney without a mattress. The surfaces were metal and very cold.

The nurses did not care to place a blanket over the cold surface to warm me up. They threw me on that piece of metal and that was it.

After the doctors set and cast my leg, they sent me to another clinic to apply stitching to my face because I had a few severe, open wounds due to the car running me over.

A couple of hours later, I was told to return to the hospital where I was admitted initially, but I adamantly refused. I was concerned about my wife, Geta. She did not know I had been hit by a car. She was sound asleep in the apartment with my three-month-old baby. I had to make it back to my apartment.

After convincing the medical staff, they told me to sign a refusal paper stating that I refused to return to the hospital. I felt compelled by God not to return to the hospital. I obeyed God's voice and was taken back to my apartment by ambulance.

A massive military officer also tagged along with us to my apartment. He carried me to my apartment.

It was already very late at night, and the communist regime shut off all the electricity throughout the apartment complex. I went into my apartment and Geta was appalled to see me in my torn clothes and blood spots on my shirt and body.

She started to cry after seeing me disfigured and badly hurt. I've never seen her so overwhelmed like this before. Geta took great care of me. She took better care of me than the doctors did in the hospital.

I eventually told Geta everything that had happened in the last several hours and she was terrified. She took care of me. I laid on my bed to rest for a bit, and I continued to tell her the story of the car accident.

I was thankful to God that he protected me. God was with me, and I felt blessed to serve a God who watches over my family and me.

The following day, the Romanian revolution began in Timișoara. It was December 16, 1989. It all started when 37-year-old László Tőkés, a Hungarian protestant assistant pastor, ignited a small protest against Nicolae Ceausescu and his mindless activities. He became an influential voice on behalf of the Timișoara community — making him a national hero and freeing the country from Vladimir Lenin's philosophy.

The rise of protesters grew in large numbers making this Romania's most serious anti-government protest in two years. This event did not happen overnight. The revolution was a massive violent crowd of protesters marching the streets of Timișoara to combat Romania's dictator — Ceausescu — and his poor economic choices.

This revolution resulted from almost two consecutive decades of food shortages, a high cost of living, no power supply, and no national freedom.

The build-up to this civil unrest started in the early 1970s when economic mismanagement occurred in Romania due to funding an oil refinery building program. This led to massive foreign debt for Romania when dictator Ceausescu relied heavily on imports to power gigantic oil refining buildings to generate energy — having borrowed money from neighboring countries.
Ceausescu also caused large amounts of destruction to Bucharest in 1977. He carried out the most devastating remodeling in Bucharest, if not the world — the removal of ancient and historical monasteries.

The dictator wanted a massive demolition of the city center. The entire Vacaresti hill had to be leveled entirely out to achieve this. Many of Bucharest's beautiful ancient churches, sports stadiums, ancient ruins, and glamorous sites were demolished. The dictator then replaced them with rows of depressing concrete apartment buildings.

He then built a tree-lined boulevard right over what used to be the Little Paris of the East — it is now all gone. There are a couple of churches rescued from this disaster by uprooting them out of the concrete and taking them to other locations. As for most of the ancient churches and monasteries, they were taken down and covered by new apartment buildings.

In the early 1980s, food exports heavily increased throughout the country when Ceausescu introduced the new austerity program, exporting cars and farm products such as meat, wheat, corn, and all sorts of food to reduce national debts. This austerity regime also caused power cuts and fuel shortages across the country. This led to the rising cost of living and food shortages that I had explained earlier.

The lines at the grocery stores increased. Food was very hard to find, and the communist regime controlled the power supply in our homes. That's not all. It keeps going.

In 1984, President Ceausescu periodically banned the use of cars for about four months to save gasoline. However, the frustration of the citizens did not stop there. Over the years, Romanian citizens all over the nation were secretly listening to Radio Free Europe/Radio Liberty station, which was illegal then. They could send you to jail just for listening, according to the communist regime. This radio station is an American-funded organization that broadcasts trending news and breaking information to European countries.

We heard about the revolutionary trend on that radio station across Europe. Countries like East Germany, Bulgaria, and Czechoslovakia had broken off from Soviet control and found national independence. This made millions of Romanian citizens furious because they also wanted to escape the Soviet communist regime.

According to the Radio Free Europe station, many communist leaders in Eastern Europe were forced to comply with democratic change demands. Ceausescu refused to comply with those regulations. In fact, he ordered that anyone who did not obey his orders be shot dead on the public streets.

This ongoing madness eventually led to a crowd of protestors seeking independence and the death of Ceausescu on the morning of December 16, 1989. Many people wanted Ceausescu dead after what he had done to our country. His philosophy was to block citizens from interacting with other European countries so that they could become brainwashed and remain under communist control.

On the early morning of December 17, 1989, things only got louder and deadlier. I woke up to loud tank blasts and constant automatic gunfire coming from the streets of Timișoara. Ceausescu summoned top communist party officials with orders to kill anyone on the streets. It didn't matter who they were or what age. Peace was no longer in the air. Screams and crying children were louder than I had ever imagined.

Geta was terrified while holding my firstborn daughter, Priscilla, in her arms. We began to pray and ask God for help because we were afraid for our lives.

An hour later, I received terrible news from one of my friends telling me that the hospital I had visited a couple of days ago from my bicycle accident had been attacked.

Dictator Ceausescu ordered that the armed forces and the Securitate reduce protesting by causing a public massacre. Communist officials marched into that hospital with rifles and killed everyone on their beds. That could have been me if I had decided to stay in that hospital because they would have thought I had participated in the protest. My heart was racing with fear. I thought, "My God, you were with me the entire time." Geta cried when she heard that news. She felt terrible pain for those who lost their lives and was glad I was still alive.

We had no choice but to stay hidden inside our apartment until those tanks were out of sight. Romania purchased those tanks from Russia. Those tanks were massive and intimidating to see in person. I would never want to come across them.

Geta desperately needed milk and bread to feed the family. Priscilla was starving, and we had run out of food. The only way to get food was at our local store a few miles from where we were staying.

I refused to let Geta go outside because of the massive killings. Geta went anyway because we had no food. She didn't want to starve to death. Bullets were flying. She couldn't believe what she saw as she walked to the store. There were dead corpses and animals on the public streets. Kids hopelessly sobbed beside their dead parents on the street, asking them to wake up.

But the worst of them all was the atmosphere of depression and loneliness that surrounded the entire city. Geta arrived back at the apartment, and we stayed hidden inside because the rage only worsened. The military troops began to make louder noises with their explosions and shootings. We became terrified for our lives in our apartment.

Soldiers were shouting at our neighbor's doors, trying to kill them. The soldiers assumed the people living in their apartments took part in the protest, but that was not true.

I took my three-year-old daughter and hid in our bedroom for safety. Anything could have happened by now. A grenade or bullets could blast through our bedroom windows at any moment. Everything was unpredictable, and I had to be the man in the home and protect my family.

I prayed to my God for help and safety because I had no control over this situation. I knew that only Jesus would have the power to keep us safe during this dangerous time. Death was right at our doorstep. I heard gunshots and people falling dead on the streets. The horrifying groans that I heard outside through my closed window were unimaginable.

Every adult male was assigned to stand outside the apartment entrance to provide extra protection. I was excused because everyone knew what had happened to my leg. I was blessed to have stayed in my room with my family, especially during the freezing cold weather.

Once the noise stopped, I felt compelled to pay a quick visit to the Metropolitan Cathedral in Bucharest. The same one that I had visited in 1973 when asking God to help me with my lathe operator final exam.

As I approached the church, I couldn't believe my eyes. What was once a remarkable and breathtaking stairway entry into a historical building was filled with dozens of dead protesters. This resulted from the deadly revolution that started in my town, happening in Bucharest.

I was scared to go inside. I stopped for a few moments and took a slow, deep breath. My stomach was not sitting right after seeing this.

No one seemed to care that dead bodies were on the ground, covered with blood and gunshot punctures. People had walked by casually. Granted, the streets were almost empty due to the deadly event. These people were fathers, mothers, children, and cousins—now gone, forever.

Again, this was life in Romania during this time. That was why I felt compelled to leave this country from day one. I knew from the start that I had to go. I needed to take action and make a move on it. There is no future for Romania, let alone for Europe.

Images and scenes began to replay in my mind. I remember when Billy Graham spoke at that cathedral years back. I could still hear the crowds chanting in my mind. I can visualize massive groups of people blowing through the streets, trying to get inside the building. I looked to my right and saw where I was standing in 1984 just before I was pushed and shoved by angry attendees.

Another scene replayed in my mind of everything that had taken place that day when I had arrived. I saw Billy Graham and his team as they arrived in Bucharest, speed-walking through the rail platform to enter the building, as people shouted and wanted to see him.

My mind replayed every scene so vividly, only to see dead corpses right in front of me — just inches away from the entrance doorway where Billy entered years ago. I felt disgusted and angry. I was sick and tired of this country. I was listening to the open-air speech that Dictator Nicolae Ceausescu made three days after the Timișoara massacre, and I realized things only got worse.

He stated that he had made a huge mistake. However, he did not take ownership of his fault and blamed others for the uprising. He intended to have a positive rally, but instead, it turned into an anti-Ceausescu demonstration. The crowds became angry, and Ceausescu fled the scene.

The following day, a Romanian senior military leader, Vasile Milea, committed suicide. The news spread everywhere. However, rumors that Ceausescu was responsible for his death went viral throughout the entire military.

The military turned against Dictator Ceausescu and joined with the protestors to kill Ceausescu and his wife, Elena Ceausescu.

Soon after that, Ceausescu feared for his life, and he and his wife went inside the Parliament of Romania, a massive building, the national bicameral legislature of Romania. A vast angry mob, including the military, surrounded the building, trying to break in.

The dictator and his wife, Elena, scrambled and swiftly escaped by exiting up through the rooftop and taking a helicopter. The military threatened to take down the aircraft with ground-to-air missiles. The pilot was forced to land on a field just forty-seven miles away from the military headquarters. The two were held in custody. Ceausescu and Elena were taken to the city of Targoviste, Romania — located in Dambovita county. They were taken to trial, which lasted only two hours. The two were accused of killing thousands of people during the revolution and were found guilty on all counts.

On Christmas Day, 1989, Dictator Ceausescu and his wife were scheduled to be sentenced to death by gunfire. Some officers planned to shoot them separately, but they were granted their last wish — to be shot and killed together.

After the trial, they were both executed by soldiers in a courtyard in Targoviste at 4 p.m. local time. That was their last Christmas, and there was a great relief in the country of Romania.

Ion Illiescu stepped forward in 1990 to run as President of Romania with the idea of maintaining the communist government. He thought that though many did not like Ceausescu, they would still like communism. Since then, there were still protests and violence even after Ceausescu's death. Shortly after President Illiescu's time in office, Romania was no longer under Soviet power.

In March 1991, the U.S. Embassy informed Geta and me that they found a sponsor from a Romanian Baptist church in Chicago. We were given a promissory contract, and I signed the contract and promised in writing that I would pay back the sponsor in due time once I arrived in the States.

On March 29, 1991, Geta, Priscilla, my newborn Patricia, and I departed Romania from the Bucharest International Airport. (Geta was pregnant with Miriam Matei while departing Romania, and she was allowed to pass through security, which was a blessing.)

From Bucharest, we landed at the Frankfurt airport in Germany, and after, we landed in New York. We filed some paperwork and legal documents at the immigration port. Finally, we were Chicago-bound. We landed and met with a fellow Romanian Christian who sponsored us.

I was living the dream I had dreamt about ever since I was a kid. God is good.

My family stayed the night at our sponsor's place until my brother-in-law, Joseph, picked us up and took us on a prolonged commute to California — we were exhausted from all the flights we had taken.

Our travel consisted of a one-night stay at a friend's house in Kansas. We slept in the car at a local gas station the other three nights. It was difficult for Geta because she was pregnant with Miriam.

God helped us, and we managed to commute to San Bernardino, California, where Geta's sister, Lana, lived. She helped Geta with diapers, food, milk, water, and shelter.

After that, Geta's other sister, Marinela, offered great hospitality to us and called her brother in Modesto, California, to get his wife, Lucia, to take us to her family.

We stayed at Lucia's home until we got settled. Eventually, we received food stamps and cash to rent an apartment. After staying at Lucia's house for over a month, we found a great deal for an apartment and immediately moved in.

Shortly after, I went to Junior College West Campus in Modesto to learn English as my second language. I graduated from the class. I did very well, so much so that the manager of that campus, Renee Peterson, offered me a position as a substitute teacher — I was shocked.

She realized I did very well based on my academic records. I politely refused.

Suddenly, I wasn't feeling well, my body was aching, and I needed to sit down for a while. She walked me to her office and started praying over me in Jesus' name. It was a very powerful prayer, too. I immediately felt much better and was amazed that Jesus healed me.

I was appreciative of this woman's obedience to pray over me. It was not common for a staff member to pray over someone else. She was courageous. She then invited my family and me to her church.

Renee was a beautiful black woman who loved the Lord. Her voice was beautiful and authoritative.

One Sunday morning, I planned to go to church, but no matter how hard I tried to get the car started, it just would not start. I called Rene and she came to my apartment and showed me to my garage.

She said, "Vio, go in your car, and I will touch your car and pray over it in Jesus' name, and you start the engine."

Immediately after she started praying, I turned the key and the car miraculously started. We were surprised. We celebrated by praising the Lord. My family was then able to drive to church that day, and I was very thankful for the hand of God over my life.

We attended Renee's church. She was the main singer that morning. She was an incredible vessel for the Lord with many talents. I was blessed to find this church because it was great for my family to attend and experience the love of God. My family took part in that church for quite some time, and we absolutely loved it.

On November 23, 1991, Miriam was born. However, this made for one of the most difficult times in our lives. When Miriam came out of the womb, her whole body was dark purple, and Geta was extremely worried and scared. The umbilical cord was wrapped tightly around her neck. There was no oxygen going to her brain. We prayed, and the doctors did everything they could to untie the cord and rescue Miriam from dying of asphyxiation. This took a while. We continued to pray until the doctors managed to remove the cord from her neck. Although the doctors removed the cord, her body was still dark, and Geta was worried. After some time, her body returned to a natural color, and everything was normal. The doctors examined Miriam's brain and miraculously found no damage to the brain or body. Praise God. I've seen the hand of God move in my family. I've learned the only way to see the great hand of God is to experience great trials and hurdles.

I believe Miriam was attacked because my spiritual enemy had an evil, strategic plan against her life. But God is greater than all evil spiritual powers. His plans will always succeed. Miriam is alive and well, currently working successfully in the medical field.

When my children were old enough to attend school, it was just a two-minute walk from our apartment. I applied for jobs, but no one would hire me because I had no work history in America. While looking for jobs, the school personnel contacted me, saying they were impressed with my children's behavior. The school knew I had five kids, so they elected me to the Parent Teacher Association (PTA).

Every month they would call me so that I could attend their meetings. I would show up, but sometimes I would stay home because I was busy looking for jobs. My family spent every night having Bible studies and prayer nights in my apartment. This was a way to honor the Lord and stay on his righteous path.

I firmly believed that God wanted to build my family up in a godly way. I wanted to be the man of the house and lead accordingly.

One day the school principal, Mr. Dumber, called begging me to attend the PTA to assist in voting for the school budget. I said I would attend. The principal delivered food and turkey that day to celebrate Thanksgiving early with the staff members. He noticed that my kids and I were very excited to see all the food delivered.

The principal felt compassion because he assumed I did not have a job and no income, and we were very hungry.

One day, the principal invited me to his office and asked me if I had a job. I said no because I have no job history in America. He told me to apply at the school district office. I had applied but did not receive a response.

So, I waited a few more days. My family and I continued to have our nightly Bible studies. Geta and I fasted from food to hear a response from Mr. Dumber.

The principal was so happy that I was invited to the main school office for an interview by the district manager, and I was offered a job on the school campus. This was a great day. I couldn't believe I was given a job so easily. I spent days looking and had terrible results. God saw how much work I put in, and He blessed me with a great job to support my family. This was incredible. This is my chance to build my work history in America.

I believe God heard my prayers and honored the Bible study nights I had with my family, so he blessed me with my first job. I strongly believe that if anyone obeys the Lord, God will reward them. I understood that fasting from food, praying, and reading the Bible daily were essential in a Christian family.

I received a follow-up call from the district manager a few days later. He mentioned that I was a dedicated and responsible man, but he needed me to work as a custodian part-time for a while. I needed a full-time position, so he also offered me a side job as a yard duty employee at a school near my residence.

Sometime after that, the principal was appointed as assistant district superintendent, a very high position in the district. He had the power to hire or fire anyone. He then came to me and offered me a full-time position as a custodian on my campus. My wife and I were very excited to hear that news. God has blessed us consistently, and we were beyond thankful. In fact, Geta was so happy that she made Romanian pastries and food for Mr. Dumber and gave them as a token of appreciation from our family.

I told him my story of what had happened in Romania and how we left the country as refugees. Mr. Dumber was heartbroken when he heard my story. He offered any help he could possibly give. He and I became great friends. He was a gift from God to me. I would not know what to do if he had not stepped into the picture with his efforts to help my family.

One day, Mr. Dumber stopped by my apartment and asked me if he could leave a lawn sign in front of my property. This sign was a small advertisement to express support for an election candidate — Mr. Dumber was running for mayor of Modesto, California.

I also donated $50 for his expenses. My family continued to pray for his success. We wanted him to be elected because he had a great heart. He was the perfect candidate for Modesto.

He supported my family with a job and food. I could only imagine how much more he could do for a city. When election day occurred, Mr. Dumber was elected. My heart melted when I heard the news, and my wife and I cried tears of joy because no one else was more worthy of being the next mayor.

Mr. Dumber and I continued to be friends for years. He remained humble throughout his entire career. That man was a positive example of how I should treat others around me.

Loyalty and kindness will help you build an excellent reputation with God and man, and Mr. Dumber is living proof of that.

I saved a large amount of money and put cash down for my first house in Modesto. That house was probably worth over $100,000 at the time. We packed our bags and moved out of the apartment. The home was located at a dead-end, cul-de-sac street. It was a two-story home with hardie board sidings for its exterior design. It was a beautiful home, and a lot of house for the money.

I still worked as a custodian and set-up crew at my local school. My manager always congratulated me for being the fastest crew member on the team, and he made me feel very good about myself. I felt like I was the employee of the month. But then, I suffered a severe back injury.

I was working at the school, tearing down the cafeteria tables. Every day I rushed to get home to see my family. This day, I lifted up a cafeteria table to fold it up, but I lifted too fast, without using my legs, and I felt tremendous pain in my lower back.

I went to my manager and told him what had happened. Being the nice guy he was, I expected him to help me keep my job, but instead, he said he didn't need me anymore. I was shocked and scared because I was out of a job and had mouths to feed.

But my close friend, Ken, helped me find a lawyer, and he arranged everything for me. We filed a lawsuit, and later, I qualified for worker's compensation. Praise God. I got paid to rest at home and get better. Talk about the ups and downs in life. I experienced them all. They're never fun, but they can take you to great places if you never give up.

My kids had the freedom to ride their bicycles around the cul-de-sac and enjoy their time. By this time, I had six children: Priscilla, Patricia, Miriam, Ruthy, Jonathan, and Sharon. They usually played outside until 9 p.m. It does not become dark until after 8:30 p.m. in California.

This was the scene I had envisioned in my mind decades ago, to see my family with no cares in the world, free to play and laugh.

Eventually, my family left Modesto, California in July 2005, because the cost of living continued to rise. We moved to Surprise, Arizona to continue living the American dream.

That was why I escaped from Romania. There was no future for that country at that time. If I had not sacrificed my time and life, my family would have stayed in Romania and suffered a lack of opportunity. Here in America, my kids went to school and received excellent grades. They have a future; they are living toward something.

People who were born in America should never take the freedom they have for granted. Someone paid for that freedom, and it can also be taken away.

I am a refugee, so I will never take this freedom for granted. I will use this freedom to contribute to the amazing American society and save money.

I pray that anyone who reads this book will become motivated to use their freedom to do great things in this country. Build businesses, write books, start a church, and get a great education. Dream big! Think big! The dream is free; putting in the work is not. God bless you for reading this amazing life story of Viorel Matei.

Books By Jonathan Matei

A family is much more than multiple biological members in a household. When members in a household provide spiritual support toward one another, they are more than roommates. God is calling all broken and lukewarm families to reunite and become whole again.

Books By Jonathan Matei

Before God created the earth, he had you in mind. He foreknew all the moments and days in your life before you were even born. Life is moving fast. Days are becoming busier and time is becoming shorter as convenience increases. Grow the right way through trying times by allowing them to shape you to be the person God has predestined you to be.

www.ingramcontent.com/pod-product-compliance
Lightning Source LLC
Chambersburg PA
CBHW030150100526
44592CB00009B/210